LIBRARIES IN BRIHAN MUMBAI

By

Dr. MANGALA B. PURANDARE
Head, Department of History
Bhavan's College
Andheri (West), Mumbai-400 058

Prof. Smt. SARITA J. MANDPE
Department of History
Bhavan's College
Andheri (West), Mumbai-400 053

Himalaya Publishing House

MUMBAI	DELHI	NAGPUR	BENGALURU	HYDERABAD	BHUBANESWAR
CHENNAI	PUNE	INDORE	AHMEDABAD	LUCKNOW	ERNAKULAM

FIRST EDITION : 2010

PUBLISHED BY : Mrs. Meena Pandey
for **HIMALAYA PUBLISHING HOUSE PVT. LTD.**
"Ramdoot", Dr. Bhalerao Marg, Girgaon, **Mumbai-400004**
☎ 23860170 • 23863863 • Fax: 022-23877178
Email: himpub@vsnl.com
Website: www.himpub.com

BRANCH OFFICES

Delhi : "Pooja Apartments", 4-B, Murari Lal Street, Ansari Road, Darya Ganj, **New Delhi-110 002.** ☎ 23270392 • 23278631 Fax: 011-23256286

Nagpur : Kundanlal Chandak Industrial Estate, Ghat Road, **Nagpur-440018** ☎ 2738731 • 3296733 • Telefax: 0712-2721215

Bengaluru : No. 16/1 (Old 12/1), 1st Floor, Next to Hotel Highlands, Madhava Nagar, Race Course Road, **Bangalore-560001.** ☎ 22281541 • 22385461 • Fax: 080-22286611

Hyderabad : No. 3-4-184, Lingampally, Beside Raghavendra Swamy Matham, Kachiguda, **Hyderabad-500027**, ☎ 040-65501745 • 09848130433

Chennai : No. 85/50, Bazullah Road, T-Nagar, **Chennai-600017**. ☎ 044-28144004 • 28144005

Pune : No. 527, "Laksha Apartment", 1st Floor, Mehunpura, Shaniwarpeth, Near Prabhat Theatre, **Pune-411030** ☎ 020-24496323 • 24496333

Lucknow : Jai Baba Bhavan, Near Dr. Sanjiv Awasthi, Church Road, Kurshi Road, Aliganj, **Lucknow-226024** ☎ 9305302158, 9415349385, 9389593752

Ahmedabad : 114, Shail, 1st Floor, Opp. Madhusudan House, C.G. Road, Navrangpura, **Ahmedabad-380009**. ☎ 079-26560126 09327324149, 09314679413

Ernakulam : No. 39/104A, Laxmi Apt., Karickamuri Cross Road, Ernakulam, **Cochin-622011.** ☎ 0484-2378012 • 2378016. 09344199799

Bhubaneswar : 5, Station Square, Bhubaneswar, Orissa-751001. 9861046007.

Indore : Kesardeep Avenue Extension, 73, Narayan Bagh, Flat No. 302, IIIrd Floor, Near Humpty Dumpty School, Narayan Bagh, **Indore (M.P.)** 99301386468

DTP by : Sudhakar Shetty (HPH Pvt. Ltd., Mumbai)

Printed by : Bhave Private Ltd., 242, Belasis Road, Nagpada, **Mumbai.**

This work is dedicated to

Late Shri Rajaram Vinayak Oturkar

and

Late Shri Govind Vitthal Patwardhan

FOREWORD

It gives me great pleasure to introduce the book "Libraries in Brihan Mumbai" What interests me is the fact that this useful compendium listing brief historical account of libraries in Mumbai, has been compiled, not by librarians, but by teachers of History, Dr. Mangala B. Purandare and Prof. Sarita J. Mandpe. It is their History subject background and their historical outlook that have given a great depth to this book, which has reached better heights than a mere directory of libraries. It will be no doubt useful as a local library directory for students of Library Science courses, as well as for library professionals. The compilers need to be sincerely congratulated for producing a really useful and comprehensive reference source on Brihan Mumbai Libraries.

Rajhansa

Prof. (Mrs.) V.P. Rajhansa
Head, D.L.I.Sc &
University Librarian
University of Mumbai.

LATE PANDIT GOVIND VITTHAL PATWARDHAN

The angel born in 1925 in a small place called Guhagar of Konkan in Maharashtra, surprised, enchanted and enthralled the pastmasters by his mastery of playing Harmonium when only 8 years old.

His passion for music was so strong that even after leaving his earthly body, his spirit prevails. Coming events show as to what he contributed to the music world.

As a young boy, after completing his formal education, he joined the Police Commissioner's office at Bombay [now the beloved Mumbai] in 1940s and after 33 years of active service he voluntarily retired, preferring to live by music and music only.

Coming into contact with maesteros of Marathi stage of the likes of Pandit Bhalchandra Pendharkar, Pandit Chhota Gandharva, Pandit Bhimsen Joshi, now Bharat Ratna, Pandit Ram Marathe, Pandit Kumar Gandharva, and all others of the likes of these supernovae of the music world [the list is endless], Panditji acquired such grandiose knowledge and expertise that his life turned into living music. He lived by music and left this world by music.

His solo renditions of Khayal Bandish, Zankar Natyageet or Bhaktigeet on harmonium were by themselves very individualistic and incomparable by the votaries of music world.

His library contained nothing, but music, music, music — in print and instruments. Engrossed so deep in his presentations that the listeners at times thought that they were listening to Kumar Gandharva, at times Ram Marathe, entirely forgetting that the Player was none else but the very soul of Pandit Patwardhan.

His every move was overshadowed by his 'peti', the humble harmonium — and it would be in good order to imagine that he was in fact not Patwardhan, but PETIWARDHAN.

What he left for posterity is beyond appreciation in any form — words or music. His contribution to music world was nothing short of a Godly Gift.

LATE RAJARAM VINAYAK OTURKAR

A time comes in the history of a country, when it presents rare personalities in various fields, be they scientists, economists, geographers, pursuers of other branches concerning life of Earth.

Rajaram Vinayak Oturkar specialized in History, Philosophy and Journalism. Educationist by profession, he devoted his entire life for History and Historical Research in India and the World.

Starting as a Lecturer at HPT College at Nashik, he moved on to Pune to teach at Bhave School and Nutan Marathi Vidyalaya before moving on to other colleges. Fifteen years thereafter, landing at K.C. College in Mumbai, he retired as founding Principal of Bombay College of Journalism.

Many a Journalists of the day recall his devotion to the art whatsoever he touched and acquired with dexterity that is uncommon any time anywhere.

The year 1932 awakened in him the spirit of Freedom to mother country, our India and gladly embraced an year's confinement behind prison bars at the hands of British rulers. He was one of the Swatantra Sainiks who evoked the rising spirit of nationalism.

Although he made Rs. 5/- per month yet he was glad to be associated and drowned in Journalism. He has penned more than 15 books on history of World, India & Maharashtra and was always concerned about making history an intercity subject of study for students of all the ages from school to college and research. Simple living and high thinking in Spartan surroundings, he was a model for the aspiring souls.

INTRODUCTION

Libraries have an important role to play in the spread of knowledge. The number of libraries in a particular city, state or country decide the level of cultural, educational and intellectual development of that city, state or that country.

So, it is very important to know about the libraries in a city like Mumbai. The city was originally an island city and soon developed with leaps and bounds, first under the British rule and later under indegenous rule. Presently, it is known as Greater Mumbai, which includes suburbs. This 'Urbs Prima in Indis' has been known for its being the capital first of the Bombay Presidency under the 'Raj' and now that of Maharashtra. Presently, it is also the commercial capital of our country. Being an important city, it has many educational institutions and libraries too.

The aim of this project is to introduce to the readers, the important libraries existing in our city. This information would help the readers, and scholars who are interested in finding information for research. This project reveals that the libraries which are 100 or more than 100 years old are mainly those which have collection of books on Humanities. They are a rich source of information about oriental and occidental studies. We find published and unpublished works in such libraries.

Libraries which are of recent origin have books of information on Modern Science, Technology, Medicine and subjects like Electronics, Computer Science and Information Technology.

While writing about the libraries we, being students of history cannot avoid the temptation of giving a brief history of each of the library included in this project.

We have divided this project in the following manner:

In the first chapter, we have given defination of the term 'Library', which includes how the concept of 'library' evolved in the world, from ancient to modern times. This includes library movement in India specially, in Mumbai.

In the second chapter, we have given a broad classification of libraries in general and have tried to follow a very simple classification of libraries. e.g., Humanities, Science & Technology. Humanities is a blanket term which covers subjects like History, Sociology, Psychology, Religion, Culture, Economics, Trade and Commerce, Entertainment, Sports and any literature connected with human culture.

Science libraries are those which devote to medical and other branches of science like Atomic Energy etc. And in Technological libraries, we have tried to give information about Indian Institute of Technology, Mumbai and others.

From the third chapter onwards we have written about each of the library which we have been able to visit or about which we have gathered information.

While collecting information on libraries, we have made use of Internet facilities also. True, the world is thinking of Wi-Fi systems, but a written word in a book form will always be available at hand in these days of power cut and non availability of electricity in many parts of our state, and in case the other systems fail due to certain reasons.

In this work, we have tried to cover maximum libraries in Brihan Mumbai. They range from the 200 year old library of the Asiatic Society, to the latest one of N.M. College, with its Cyber-cafe and Wi-Fi-system. We were not able to cover many more libraries like Libraries of Reserve Bank,

I.C.I.C.I. or the American Centre Library, or the Library of Maxmuller Bhavan due to paucity of time. But we have tried to cover at least one from each category.

While collecting information, we had the opportunity to discuss certain issues with the librarians and the library staff. We have made the following observations.

1. Libraries run by Public Trusts face financial crunch. As such maintenance and conservation of the rare collections as well as purchase of new books becomes a problem.
2. Non-availability of sufficient funds also results in poor/part payment to staff leading to lack of enthusiasm for routine work.
3. Age old rules about home issue of books lead to poor readership of valuable and rare books. (working students cannot manage to spend long hours in the library)
4. Sophisticated libraries with proper funding are in a position to provide facilities like photo copies of the text, on line information, on line Resource sharing etc.
5. College students prefer to read Newspapers and Magazines, rather than going to the stacks for reference work. On the other hand students of Professional courses prefer to have libraries 24 hours Monday to Sunday.
6. Libraries in certain localities, provide special facilities to students of the area during exam time. Examination time e.g., Kamlabai Nimbkar Library, Khar (West).
7. To attract more readers, some libraries arrange activities like book fair, lecture series, fellowships,

documentaries etc. A few libraries have their own publication departments. e.g., MMGS.

8. Most of the Research libraries are located in South Mumbai while the readers reside in the suburbs. Improper travelling conditions prevent them from making optimum use of these libraries.
9. Today's generation lacks enthusiasm for such activities as establishment of libraries, may be because of the availability of information with a click. Earlier, as in the case of some of the libraries like MMGS, Dadar Sarvajanik Vachanalaya etc. the youngsters had taken efforts to collect money, books etc. to start libraries.

In conclusion we say that the development in information technology has provided advantages of storing data from and about documents/rare material in machine readable form. This will have impact on information gathering customs of the future. And on, one day the contents of the greatest libraries in the world will be at the fingertips of the people, in their own offices or home. We strongly feel that more and more libraries should be established in the suburbs of Mumbai or Brihan Mumbai.

However, this does not mean that libraries as institutions will cease to exist. On the contrary they will become more accessible and popular. After all, a written word has no alternative.

We hope our efforts will be helpful to scholars and would not appear as foolhardy undertaking.

Dr. Mangala B. Purandare
Prof. Sarita Mandpe

ACKNOWLEDGEMENT

In preparation of this Research Project, we have received invaluable help from institutions and individuals. We wish to acknowledge our indebtedness to them.

First and foremost we owe a debt to the U.G.C. for sanctioning this project and allotting funds for the same. We would like to record our thanks to Dr. Smt. Indu Kulkarni, Ex-Principal of our college (Bhavan's College, Andheri (W), Mumbai-400 058.) who forwarded the proposal for this project to U.G.C. and encouraged us to undertake it. We would also like to thank Dr. Smt. V.I. Katchi, the Principal of our college for her cooperation.

Our thanks are due to all the Librarians and Library-staff of the Libraries which are covered in this project. Each one of them was extremely cooperative but the paucity of space prevents us from writing names of each one of them.

However, we owe a lot to Ms. Shubhangi Gavankar (Wilson College), Ms. Vaishali Davar (N.M. College), Prof. Vijaya Rajhans (University of Mumbai), Dr. R.M. Dave and Dr. K.K.C. Lakshmi Narsimhan (Anantachari Institute), Ms. Sneha Bagwe and Santosh Pange (Mumbai Marathi Granthasangrahalaya), Dr. Sonal Shukla and Dr. Kumudben (Vacha), Smt. Manju Trivedi (Indian Merchants Chamber), Ms. Gulshan Cooper (People's Free

Reading Room and Library), Ms. Nirupama (Nalanda Nrityakala Academy), Shri. Hanif Mohammad Nalkhandi, Shri. Salam Saheb Tungekar, Shri. Shabbir Chohan, Shri. Shashikant Jesrani, Shri Rashidbhai (Kutub Khana), Prof. Smt. Archana Calangutcar (Dept. of History, Bhavan's College, Andheri), Shri. Ramesh Paloti (Bhavan's College, Andheri), and Smt. Manisha Samant (Former Asst. Librarian, Bhavan's College, Andheri) and the staff of Saraswati Granthaghar of Bharatiya Vidya Bhavan, All of them have taken great pains to read, our work and give suggestions.

We are grateful to Smt. Pramodtai and Parag and our other family members who have constantly encouraged us in our work and helped us to complete it.

Our special thanks to Principal Dr. Vasanti Katchi and her sister Smt. Kalindi Sathaye for their financial support for the publication of this work.

Last but not the least, we are thankful to Ms. Saloni and Smt. Deepa Shinde for the computer work.

— Dr. Mangala B. Purandare

— Prof. Sarita Mandpe

CONTENTS

1

'LIBRARY' AND LIBRARY MOVEMENT

WHAT IS LIBRARY?

Library is a collection of books and related material for use by the public or by members of a group. It can also be a person's collection of books. It can be a room or building containing a collection of books (for reading or reference rather than for sale). It can be a collection of films, records, computer routines etc.[1]

According to yet another source, Library means books to consult and borrow.[2]

A third source gives a more detailed and perhaps the latest meaning of the term 'Library'. It says, " A Library is a collection of information resources and services, organized for use, and maintained by a public body, institution, or private individual. In the more traditional sense, it meant a collection of books. This collection and services are used by people who choose not to or cannot afford to — purchase an extensive collection themselves, who need material no individual can reasonably be expected to have, or who

1. *D. K. Illustrated Oxford Dictionary,* originally published in 1998 by Dorling Kindersley Limited and Oxford University Press, Great Britain, 2003 edition, p. 406.
2. Ruth Binney, (ed.), *Reader's Digest, The Origins of Everyday Things,* Reader's Digest Association Limited, London, 2002, p. 227.

require professional assistance with their research."[3] The same source further says, "However, with the collection of media other than books for storing information, many Libraries are now also repositories and access points for maps, prints or other documents and artworks on various storage media such as micro film, microfiche, audio tapes CDs, LPs, cassettes, video tapes and DVDs and provide public facilities to access CD-ROM and subscription databases and the Internet."[4]

Thus, modern libraries are redefined as places to get unrestricted access to information in many formats and from many sources.

More recently, libraries are understood as extending beyond the physical walls of a building, by including material accessible by electronic means, and by providing the assistance of Librarians[5] in navigating and analyzing tremendous amounts of knowledge with a variety of digital tools.

Thus, the term library has acquired a secondary meaning "a collection of useful material for common use", and in this sense is used in fields such as computer science, mathematics and statistics, electronics and biology.

HISTORY

From when do we find libraries in India? The discovery of innumerable seals at Mohenjodaro, Harappa, Lothal and other places confirm the fact that writing was well-known in Pre-historic India.[6]

---

3. Wikipedia. org/wiki/Library, p. 1.
4. *Ibid*
5. Librarians are the specialists who are experts in matters related to finding and organizing information and interpreting information needs.
6. Kumar P.S.G., A student's manual of Library and Information Science, p. 112.

By 700 B.C. universities or centres of learning were started in Panchala, Kuru, Videha, Matsya,Usinara, Takshashila (Taxila) Nimisharanya, Kasi and other places. Acharya Nagarjuna, the scholar of Mahayan Buddhism is known to have maintained a library on the top floor of the University building at Takshashila. Takshashila was one of the most important seats of learning in Ancient India. Teaching here was mostly Vedic literature, Philosophy and 18 shilpas. It is recorded that there was a rich library at this place. The great grammarian Panini and great economist Kautilya were students of this university.[7]

Another important library of great significance was that of Nalanda University in 4th century A.D. Nalanda the most famous of all, was respected for its scholarship all over India. To have been to Nalanda was a hallmark of culture. It was not easy to enter it. Admission was restricted to those who had already attained a certain standard. It specialized in postgraduate studies and attracted students from China, Japan, Tibet, Korea, Mongolia and Bokhara. Apart from religious and philosophical subjects (both Buddhist and Brahmanical) secular and practical subjects were also taught. There were schools of arts, a department of architecture, medical school, an agricultural department and dairy farms. The intellectual life of the university is said to have been one of animated debates and discussions. The spread of Indian culture abroad was largely the work of scholars from Nalanda."[8] Naturally such a renowned

7. Nehru Jawarlal, *The Discovery of India,* p. 117 metions 'It was considered an honour and distinction to be a graduate of Taxila. Physicians who had studied in the school of medicine were highly thought of, and it is relented that whenever, Buddha felt unwell, his admirers brought to him a famous physician who graduated from Taxila. Panini, the great grammarian of the sixth-seventh century B.C. is said to have studied there.'

8. *Ibid,* p. 223.

university had well equipped libraries. The entire area where library buildings existed was known as 'Dharma Ganj' or Mast of religion. There were three library buildings in this area. These buildings were known 'Ratna Sagar', Ratna Dadhi and Ratna Ranjaka.[9] Ratna Ranjaka was a nine storied building while others were six storied.

Other important academic libraries of ancient India were Odantapuri, Somapuri, etc. Jawaharlal Nehru mentions, ..."there were many centres of cultural and philosophical thought and every person who advanced a new theory or new interpretation of an old theory, had to come there to justify himself. Kashmir was for long, a great Sanskrit centre of Buddhist and Brahmanical learning. The great universities flourished............Then there was Vikramashila University, near modern Bhagalpur in Bihar and Valabhi in Kathiawar. During the period of Guptas, Ujjayini university rose prominence. In the south there was Amravati University."[10] These Universities had libraries of their own.

Ancient period was followed by the medieval period. Many medieval rulers were patrons of education, learning and literature. They had developed libraries. Babur, the founder of Mughal rule in India, is said to have brought with him all the specimens he could collect from library of his ancestors. He, himself was a well known scholar and had authored many books. His autobiography 'Tuzuki Baburi', written in Turkish language is the best example of his scholarship. It is a very important source of medieval

---

9. Pt. Mahadevshastri Joshi, (Ed.) *Bhartiya Sanskriti Kosh (*Mar.) (Vol. V), p. 78. However, Tarkatirtha Lakshmanshastri Joshi, (ed.) Marathi Vishwa Kosh, (Vol. VIII) p. 545 names are mentioned as Ratnasagar, Ratnoday and Ratnaranjaka.
10. Nehru Jawaharlal, *op.cit.,* p. 223.

Indian history.[11] Babur's son Humayun was also a lover of books and it is said that he converted a pleasure house in Purana Quila in Delhi into a library.

Akbar, the next ruler, had maintained an imperial library and Mulla Pir Muhammad was his librarian. The books in his library were classified and catalogued according to a scheme that was developed by the scholars of the time. Akbar had established a separate department for translation and illustration of Manuscripts.[12]

Interestingly, Jehangir is said to have maintained a personal library, which moved with him where ever he went.

Aurangzeb also encouraged libraries and Islamic learning. The Mughal period of Indian history was followed by the British period also known as Raj or modern period of Indian history. The Portuguese were already in India, specially in Goa, The Christian missionaries were responsible for the introduction of printing press in India. The first press was established on September 6, 1556 A.D. It was brought from Portugal by accident. Originally it was to be sent to Abyssinia, but landed in Goa and by that time the relations between the Portuguese and Abyssinian ruler were strained and the press was retained in Goa.[13]

The English East India Company had established fort St. David Library at Cuddalore in 1707 A.D. In the year 1709 A.D., the society for Promotion of Christian knowledge sent circulating Library at Calcutta, the first of its kind in India.[14]

11. Pt. Mahadevshastri Joshi, *Bhartiya Sanskriti Kosh,* (Vol. VIII) p. 513.
12. Kumar P.S.G., *op. cit,* p. 114.
13. Priyalkar & others, *Pancharati* (Mar.), p. 2.
14. Kumar P. S. G., *op. cit,* p. 115.

The Royal Asiatic Society was established at Calcutta in 1784 A.D. Its started Asiatic researches, and a journal in 1787 A.D.

The British introduced an exotic concept of Public Libraries by starting few of those in chief metropolitan cities of India, in the late 18th century. Before this, there were libraries but they were purely private. Some of them were owned by the native rulers, or their officials. These libraries were not for public use. Only a few people had access to those.[15]

The British felt the need for libraries after establishing their settlements in different parts of India. The British residents of Calcutta made an appeal to the society for Promotion of Christian Knowledge to dispatch a 'Circulating Library' for them. The society therefore, sent one such library in 1709. From this time onwards the idea of library for all, developed in India. Fort St. George Library was established in 1714 A.D. East India Company's Library was established in 1715 A.D. in Bombay and a similar one was established at Calcutta too.[16]

English East India Company faced administrative difficulties due to language barriers. To solve the problem, the company established schools to train local people. The company also needed native scholars to learn British system of administration and Law. They wanted to train them to act as middlemen between the Company and the people. So, later, they also established institutions imparting higher education to Indians. Thus, the first three modern

15. *Ibid,* Priyalkar & others, *op.cit.*, p. 9, mention that the foundations of the Library Movement in India were laid by Captian P.T. French of 23rd Native Infantary in1838 at Ahemadnagar.
16. Kumar P.S.G., *op.cit,* p. 115.

universities were established in Bombay, Calcutta and Madras. These Universities were equipped with libraries.[17]

This was followed by the establishment of Research Libraries in India, like, The Royal Asiatic Society, Calcutta and The Bombay Branch of the Royal Asiatic Society, the library of the University of Bombay (now Mumbai) and the like.

Here, we cannot avoid the temptation of writing briefly about the library movement in rest of the world.

As far as the world is concerned, the early libraries were partly libraries. They had unpublished records, which are usually viewed as archives and not libraries. Archaeological findings from the ancient city states of Sumer have revealed temple rooms full of clay tablets in cuneiform script. These were records of commercial transactions or inventories. Few of them referred theological matters, historical events and legends.

One of the greatest discoveries of cuneiform inscriptions was the first millennium B.C. library of king Assurbanipal at Nineveh, the capital of Assyria excavated in 1850's by British archaeological team. Its 25000 odd tablets and fragments are inscribed with bilingual Summerian Akkadian texts, literary and religious works, incantatious and letters, as well as, with diverse astronomical, medieval and lexicographical writings. The King got his scribes to copy and collect tablets from all over his kingdom. It remains to this day the most important single collection of cuneiform material ever found.[18] Things were much the same in the government and temple records

17. *Ibid.*
18. Samuel Noah Kramer and the editors of *Time-Life* books, Great Ages of Man, A Historyof the Worlds Culture, Cradle of Civilization.

on papyrus of Ancient Egypt. Library existed in both Babylonia and Egypt before 2000 B.C. Founded in the 3rd century B.C. at Alerxandria in Egypt, the largest Greek library reputed to have held as many as 700000 scrolls.

Private or personal libraries made up of non-fiction and fiction books appeared in classical Greece. The first one appeared sometime near the 5th century B.C. The book collectors of Hellenistic Antiquity were listed in the late second century in Deipnosophista — "Polycrates of Samos and Pisistratus who was tyrant of Athens, and Nicorrates of Samos and even the kings of Pergamos, and Euripides the poet and Aristotle the philosopher, and Nelius his librarian from whom they say our country men Ptolemane's surnamed Philadelphus, brought them all and transported them with all those which he had collected at Athens and the Rhodes to his own beautiful Alexanderia.[19] All these libraries were Greek; the cultivated Hellenized diners in Deipnosophitae pass over the libraries of Rome in silence. At Villa at Herculaneum the Villa of Ceasar's father-in-law the Greek library has been perserved in volcanic ash. Archaeologists are of the opinion that a Latin library kept separate from the Greek one can be discovered at the site.

Libraries were filled with parchment scroll as at Pergumum and on papyrus scroll as at Alexanderia. This library and private libraries were open to an educated public but it is believed that they had no direct access to the stacks.[20]

Little is known about early Chinese libraries. It is recorded that imperial library was established during the time of Qin dynasty. At another place it is recorded that

19. http;//en nikipedia. org/wiki/library, p. 2.
20. *Ibid.*

one of the curators of the imperial library in the Han Dynasty is said to have been the first to establish a library classification system and the first book notation system. The library catalog was written on scrolls of fine silk and these scrolls were stored in silk bags.[21]

Persian kings and Zoroastrian elite had established libraries in Persia. A Royal library in Isfahan was among the first one in Persia One of the most important public libraries established around 666 A.D. in South-western Iran, was the library of Gundishapur.

In the West, the first public libraries were established under Roman Empire. Each of the Roman emperor tried to establish a library much better than the one started by the earlier emperor. Readers had direct access to the scrolls. These scrolls were kept on the shelves built into the walls of a large room. People could read and write in the same room. It is recorded that at time books were borrowed by the public. Roman public libraries were bilingual, Latin and Greek.

It is recorded, "Cassidorus, Minister to Thedoric, established a monastry at Vivarium in the heel of Italy with a library where he attempted to bring Greek learning to Latin readers and preserve text both sacred and secular for future generations. As its unofficial librarians, Cassidorous, not only collected as many manuscripts as he could, he also wrote treatises aimed at instructing his monks in the proper uses of reading and method for copying texts

21. *Ibid.*

accurately. In the end however, the library at Vivarium was dispersed and lost within a century."[21]

After the fall of the Western Roman Empire and before the rise of the large Western Christian Monastry libraries beginning at Montecassino, libraries were found in few places in the 'Christian Middle East'.

With the rise of Islam, libraries in newly Islamic countries, developed in Middle East, North Africa, Sicily and Spain. They had books of modern type and not the scrolls. These books were made of paper, Books could also be found in Mosques and sponsored public libraries. Unfortunately, Islamic libraries of the present times, do not hold these antique books. Many were lost, destroyed by Mongols or Spanish Inquistors or removed to European libraries during the colonial period.[22]

By the ninth century public libraries began to appear in many Islamic cities. They were called 'Halls of Science' (dar al-ilm) These libraries were endowed by Islamic sects for some reasons. One was to spread secular knowledge and ideas. These libraries employed translators and copyists in large numbers in order to get Persian, Greek and Roman non-fiction and the classics translated into Arabic. After a few centuries, as said earlier, these libraries were victims of wars and religious strife in the Islamic world. However, a few examples of these medieval libraries, such as the libraries of Chinguetti in West Africa remain, intact and relatively unchanged even today.[23]

---

21. *Ibid,* p. 3.
22. John L. Esposito (ed), The Oxford Encyclopedia of Modern Islamic World, Cup (1995).
23. Wikipedia P3. The same source also states that another library from this period which is still operational and expanding is the central library of Astan Quads Razavi in the Iranian city of Mashhad which is functioning for more than six centuries.

The contents of these Islamic libraries were copied by scholars in Christian border areas, specially from Spain and Sicily. The resulting conglomerate libraries are the basis of every modern library today.

The earliest examples in England of a library which was for non members of a Cathedral or college was the Francis Trigge Chained Library in Grantham, Lincolnshire. It was established in 1598. The Library exists even at present. It is the forerunner of the later public library system.

In 1602 A.D., in England, the diplomat Sir Thomas Bodley restored a medieval library in Oxford. Eight years later, the government's publishing body, the Stationer's company, resolved to give the Bodleians a copy of every new book published in Britain. The British Museum Library, now the British library, was awarded the same privilege in 1753 A.D.[24]

During the 18th and 19th centuries subscription lending libraries flourished. Some still survive, such as the London Library, founded in 1841 A.D. Free Public libraries were established by Act of Parliament in 1850.[25]

As the concept of libraries developed in the world, there was progress of library architecture for the need of security of books. Buildings with well-lit rooms and provision for lecturers, armaria or shelves were built.[26]

TYPES OF LIBRARIES

Libraries can be divided into categories by several methods. They are mentioned below:

24. Reader's Digest, *op.cit.*
25. *Ibid.*
26. books were chained to lecterns or shelves.

(1) By the entity that supports or maintains them.[27]

(*i*) Tribal Libraries

(*ii*) School Libraries

(*iii*) Private Libraries

(*iv*) Corporate Libraries

(*v*) Government Libraries

(*vi*) Academic Libraries

(*vii*) Historical Society Libraries

(2) By the Type of documents they hold:

(*i*) Digital Libraries[28]

(*ii*) Data Libraries

(*iii*) Photographic Libraries

(*iv*) Slide Libraries

(*v*) Tool Libraries

(3) By the subject matter of documents they have:

(*i*) Architecture Libraries

(*ii*) Fine arts Libraries (Music Libraries)

(*iii*) Law Libraries

(*iv*) Medical Libraries

(*v*) Military Libraries

(*vi*) Theological libraries.

---

27. By entity it means institution Municipality or any corporated body.
28. Rakesh L.B., Library and The Information Science in Digital Age, p. 224.

    Digital library is a new concept. It explains the nature of its collection. Digital library is an electronic library in which large number of geographically distributed users can access the contents of large and diverse repositories of electronic objects like - network text, image, maps, sounds, videos, catalogues of merchandise, scientific knowledge, and so on. Such a library is understood to have the information stored predeominantly in electronic or digital medium like digital books, digital or scanned images, graphics, textual or numeric data, digitalized films, audio and video clips etc.

(4) By users they serve

(*i*) Military communities.

(5) Traditional and professional divisions[29]

(i) Academic Libraries: These libraries are on the campuses of colleges and universities. They are mainly for the students and staff as well as other academic institutions. Some academic libraries like the library of the University of Mumbai, are accessible to general public as a whole.

(ii) School libraries: Most of Public and Private, Primary and Secondary Schools have libraries which are equipped with the books to support school syllabus, curriculum, etc.

(iii) Research Libraries: These libraries take care of supporting scholarly research. They maintain permanent collection and most of them provide access to all necessary material. Research libraries are academic or national libraries. Many libraries have research facilities within their special field. Asiatic society's library can be described as Research library

(v) Public libraries or public lending libraries: These libraries cater to the needs of general public. Some of the books from such libraries are meant for borrowing. Readers can borrow those for a period of days or weeks. These libraries issue cards to the members for such purpose. These libraries sometimes serve as community organizations that provide free services and events to the public e.g., Mumbai Marathi Grantha Sangrahalaya is a

29. *wikipedia,* pp. 1-3.

library which conducts lectures on literature for public, it publishes books also.[30]

(v) **Special libraries:** All other libraries fall into this category. Such libraries are maintained by private and public organisations including hospitals, museums, research laboratories, law firms. Many government departments and agencies have libraries to be used by their employees in doing specialized research related to their work. Thus, special library is restricted in its collection and also the number of users it serves and are small in size.[31]

Special library is a new concept beginning in 20th century when number of organisations felt the need to collect documents to satisfy their special interest. General Libraries were not much useful to them.

Special library recognized the 'Value of Ranganathan's law' — 'Save the time of users, right material to the right person at the right time'.

Librarian in a special library has the knowledge of the subject.[32]

But the simplest division of liabraries is circulating libraries and collecting libraries.[33]

Many modern libraries are a combination of the two. General collection of such libraries is for circulation Reference collection is more specialized and it is restricted to library premises only, it cannot be taken out of the library. The libraries mentioned in this project are listed in alphabetical order of their names.

30. Response to questionnaire by the librarian of MMGS. However, this is a reference library only.
31. *wikipedia,* pp. 1-3.
32. Kumar P.S.G., *op.cit.,* p. 124.
33. Cirulating library is the one where materials are intended to be loaned to patrons, institutions collecting libraries are those where material and other liabraris are selected on a basis of their subject matter.

2

AKHIL HIND MAHILA PARISHAD'S LIBRARY

This library was established in 1977. Smt. Binduben Pandit, Giraben Meheta, Induben Dalal, Kusumben Dalal and others were its founder members. Lion's club of Vile Parle East provided the necessary funds to establish it.

This library is devoted to Gujarati literature i.e., Novels, Short Stories, Essays. There are about 6500 books of this kind. The library adds about 100 to 150 books every year.

Any one who can read and understand Gujarati can become members. This is a public library.

It is located at Vile Parle East, near East West bridge.

3

ANANTACHARYA INDOLOGICAL RESEARCH INSTITUTE'S LIBRARY (AIR)

This is an Indological Research Institute. It is named after the great Vaishnava Anantacharya and it was inspired by Dr. K.K.A. Venkatachari, members of Somani Family (B.D. and G.D. Somani) and Sri Venkatesh Devasthan, Phanas wadi, Girgaon, Mumbai.[1] The Somanis provided a single large accommodation and other infrastructural facilities for the library and Research centre in 1974 at G.D. Somani school building at Cuffe Parade Mumbai. Dr. S.G. Mudgal, Dr. N.A. Deshpande, Dr. V.S. Nayar, Dr. H.S. Thosar and Dr. Y.S. Walimbe helped Dr. K.K.A. Venkatachari, to develop the institute.[2]

Jagadguru Gadi Anantacharya after whom the institute is named, had a dream of bringing up an ideal reference library and a research Institute for scholars. Accordingly the library was established along with the

This information is made available to us as a response to our questionnaire.

1. Sri. U. Ve. P.B. Anantacharya of Kanchi was a great savant of shrivashnavism, who lived during the years 1874-1936. He was a great sanskrit Scholar. He was known as Jagadguru Gadi Ananthacharya swami. He was a great lover of books and he had a huge personal library of books and manuscripts in Srivaishanvism, other vaishnava Sampradayas, scriptures and different branches of Indian Philosophy and Hindi Culture
2. Information provided by the Director of the Institute.

Institute in 1974. It is recognised by University Grants Commission and affiliated to the University of Mumbai.

This library is open to all scholars. It has a valuable collection of 14,493 printed volumes on various subjects such as Sanskrit literature, Philosophy, Culture, Science, Indian History, Art architecture, Sculpture, Painting, Dance, Archaeology, Numismatics, Iconography and Epigraphy. Besides these, there are journals like Indian Culture, Indian Historical Quarterly, Epigraphia India, Poona Orientalist, Journal of Tamil Studies Annuals of Bhandarkar Oriental Research Institute, A.S.I. Reports, Puranas (Published by Kashiraj Trust – Varanasi) Brahmavidya (Published by Theosophic society Adyar, Madras) Annuals of Oriental Research, Madras, Journal of Indian History, Journal of Oriental Institute, Varodara Bulletin of the Institute of Traditional Culturers, Madras and special issues of Kalyan.[3]

Besides the printed volumes and journals there is a precious collection of 800 Palm Leaf manuscripts on different topics in the languages Sanskrit, Tamil and Manipravala, represented in Grantha, Telugu, Tamil and Devanagari Scripts.

The topics covered by manuscripts include Vedic Samhitas, Epics, Upanishadas, Vedanta, Dharmashashtra, Samskaras, Kavya Kosa, Poetics, Stotras, Mantras, Jyotishya, Ganita and Medicine.[4]

These manuscripts are well preserved with; the periodical application of lemon grass oil and fumigation. All manuscripts are catalogued and listed. The Institute wants to publish some selective manuscripts. It is the chief conservator of manuscripts.[5]

This institute is at G.D. Somani Memorial School Building, Cuffe Parade, Mumbai-400 005. Phone: 22184174.

3. *Ibid*
4. Ibid Cuffe Parade Colaba Express, p. 18
5. Indian Express, Mumbai Newsline, Wednesday 9 the May, 2001.

4

ANJUMAN: ISLAM URDU RESEARCH INSTITUTE LIBRARY

On 21st February, 1874, a number of enlightened Muslims of Mumbai, joined together and formed themselves into an association and named it Anjuman-i-Islam.[1] Right from its inception, the association tried to provide opportunities and facilities to the Muslim community. The Association opened its school on 20th September, 1880 in Mumbai. Thus it started playing an important role in the education of Muslims.

Besides establishing a school, later, in 1947 it started the Urdu Research Institute. This Institute is in affiliation to the University of Mumbai. Kazi Abdul Karim Porbandari donated 4418 valuable books in Arabic, Persian, Urdu, English and other, languages to Anjuman-i-Islam. With this collection the Urdu Research Institute's library began functioning. Hence, this library is called Karimi Library. This library has reference section and lending section. Some rare collections housed in this library are:

Diwan-e-Arafi, Bustan-e- Saadi, Works of Ghalib, Kushafi's Anwar-e-Arafi, Anwar-e-Saheli and Fauz-e-al-Kabir Ma'fathi-al-Nazir.[2]

This library is located at Anjuman-i-Islam Urdu Research Institute, D.N. Road, Mumbai - 400 001.

1. Desnavi S.S., The Anjuman-i-Islam: A century old Institute p. 1.
2. Bijle S.M., Library Facilities for Research in Urdu, Arabic and Persian Languages, and literture, in the city of Mumbai, (Greater Bombay), unpublished dissertation for M.Lib. University of Mumbai p. 62.

5

ASIATIC SOCIETY'S LIBRARY

Lord Mountstuart Elphinstone, the Governor of Bombay, took interest in introducing new and modern thoughts in India. This led to the establishment of educational societies and libraries. British offers used to meet in club in Hornmon circle. They established the literary society, which led to the foundation of Asiatic Society.

In 1804 A.D., 17 eminent British founded the Literary society of Bombay. The aim was to enlighten people. It established a meteorological laboratory, besides those for physics and chemistry. To collect money for establishment of library, the society arranged for a lottery, with government permission. The money that was raised was used to build the Town Hall. The government also gave some grants, Sir James Mackintosh took lot of efforts. The place for the Town Hall was at Bombay Green. The building was ready in 1833 A.D.[1]

The Library Society was renamed as Bombay Branch of Royal Asiatic society. In the early days this society was for the British only. A person had to be selected for membership, which was Rs. 60. The fees have been altered many times. Today, the life membership is Rs. 10,000.

1. Acharya Shingne, *Mumbaicha Vruttanta* (Marathi), pp. 267-268.

The Asiatic Society is well-known for its library. It has books from Agro Horticulture society, Geographical Society, Medical Physical Society's Library. Some British officers gave their personal collection of books and manuscripts, to the Library.[2]

According to the Annual Report of 1994-95 the library had 2, 31,489 books, on subject like Sanskrit, Political Science, Ethics, Law, Travelogues, biographies, auto biographies, Geography etc.

The Library is specially useful for Oriental studies.

The library has a wide collection of books on flora, fauna, life paintings, archaeology, Vastushastra and culture. The following works are to be specially noted.

1. Achilles Tatrus — published in 1640.
2. Galileo Galilie
3. History of the World by Sir Waller Raleigh
4. Birds of Asia by John Gold.
5. William Shakespeare: works ed. Charles Knights
6. Rajtarangini of Kalhana

The Divine Comedy written by Dante and Shahnama by Firdausi are the prized Jewels of this library. Secondly, the library has preserved manuscripts like Bhagwat Purana, Kalpasutras and Vikramcharita, which belongs to 12th century.

The Society gives Justice Chhagla scholarship to research student. It also publishes research work in its own journal. The society gives the Campbell Gold medal

2. Madgaonkar G. N., Mumbaiche Varnan (Marathi).
Other information is based on article in Mumbai Times (Marathi) 23, November 2003, Sakal (Marathi) 18, Nov. 2004.

and Mahamahopadhyay Dr. P.V. Kane Gold medal and the Society's Gold medal to research scholars.

The library aims at preserving the valuable collection. It has its own microfilming center. The catalogues are computerised.

Funds were and are needed from time to time. In the past, people like Jagannath Shankarseth, Jamshedji Tata, Premchand Roychand, Cawasji, Jahangir, Dinshaw Petit donated thousands of rupees to this library. Recently, the State government too, has promised funds for the library.

The government of Maharashtra has promised funds to the Asiatic Library.

The library is open to member researchers. From Monday to Saturday.

6

AWAMI IDARAH LIBRARY

This is the best example of a library which was started by social workers for the people staying in Mominpura, Byculla West. Most of the people in this area have economic problems and the children in this area are unable to get proper education. The mill workers of this area started Awami Idarah in 1951.[1] The library was also established in the same year. It has 10,000 books and periodicals. These books were donated by various institutions and individuals. There is no special budget or funds for this library nor is there any librarian, yet it functions very smoothly with the help of volunteers.[2]

This library is included here for scholars who take interest in social welfare and social work. It provides a model of social upliftment without any help from government.

This library is open to all in the area where it is located.

This library is at Mominpura, Byculla (West), Mumbai.

1. Bijle M., *op.cit.*, p. 69.
2. *Ibid*.
   The information about this library is received from the librarian in response to the questionnaire.

7

BHARATIYA VIDYA BHAVAN'S SARASWATI GRANTHAGHAR

There are more than 80,000 books in this library which was established by Dr. K.M. Munshi the Kulapati of Bharatiya Vidya Bhavan. There are many rare works in Sanskrit dedicated to literature and 'Dharmashashtra.'

One finds epics in Sanskrit, Four Vedas, Upanishads, 18 Puranas, Smritis, the commentaries on Vedas all the works of the famous Sanskrit scholars like Kalidasa are preserved here.

Works of Ptolemy, Hu-en-Sang, Dhammapadas, Tripitikas and many other works in Prakrit, Pali and Ardhamagadhi are among the rich collections of this library.

Shabdachintamani, a work in Sanskrit, Vaidik Kosh, Abhinav Rajendra Kosh are some of the rare books in this library. Besides these, there are well-known works in Hindi, Marathi, Gujarati, Sanskrit, Prakrit, Pali, Bengali, Ardhamagadhi and in other Indian languages.

Books on Art, Architecture, Sculpture, History of India as well as that of the world, Philosophy (Indian and Western) Logic, Music, travellers' accounts are available here.

One finds very rare works of 16th century on history and Sanskrit. e.g., Malabar and Coromandal by Jones published in 1672 A.D. Another book gives detailed information of weights, measures and coins. It is entitled as Numismana Orientalia. This book is written by Edward Thomas.

'Les Hindus' the book written in French by Tome Premier in the 18th century is found here in a very good condition.

The natural history of animals written by Karl Vohite and Frederick Stheket, published in 1889 is another valuable book preserved here. Magic, the book written by Albert Hopkins in 1897 keeps the readers attracted to this library. Green's Views in India in the Times of Sepoy of Mutiny, a newspaper sized book on 1857 Revolt, published in 1859 is a valuable possession of this library 'Sandhya', the book on daily worship rituals of the Brahmins is written by S.C. Belongs, in 1851 is among the valuables in this library.

G.K. Chesterton's 'Famous paintings' a book of copy of painting of the world is also available for reference in this library, along with many volumes of the Journal of Indian Art, Grammer of Ornaments written in 1910, giving information about the ornaments in India and 'Coins of the Jews published in 1903.

There are books written in Marathi for example Marathi Vishvakosh (Lakshamnashashtri Joshi) Ketkar's Maharashtriya Shabdakosh, BhagvatiMandal a Vishwakosh in Gujarati, Hindi, Sanskrit and Pali dictionaries, Encyclopedia Britanica, Moropant's entire works (1916) Imperial Gazetteers, George Wat's Dictionary of Economic Products of India Published in 1891 A.D. in six volumes,

Dr. P.V. Kane's History of Dharmashastra Indian Culture in 10 Volumes, the Cultural Heritage of India, Encyclopedia of Religion ethics in of volumes are in the collection of this library.

Besides these rare books, there are water colour paintings of medieval period. However, the star attraction of this library is its collection of manuscripts. Ancient manuscripts are a cultural treasure of perennial value. The value of a manuscript lies not only in its content but also in its original form and appearance. The external appearance of the manuscript throws light on the chronological status of the manuscript. It bears the strength of original evidence in the disputes of history and helps to settle them finally. Bharatiya Vidya Bhavan has a collection of 1377 paper manuscripts and 27 palm-leaf manuscripts. These manuscripts pertain to as many as twenty-six subjects in different languages.

There is a manuscript of Mahabharata in the form of a big roll of 30 c.m. diameter and 15 c.m. width. It is written on a very thin paper pasted on a thin cloth. The writing is extremely minute. It cannot be deciphered without the help of a magnifying glass. Along with the text, there are illustrative paintings. To add to the beauty of this work, there appears decorative golden borders on both sides. It is a work of a single hand. Such innovation in calligraphy is rare. This manuscript seems to be from Rajasthan. Descriptive catalogue of manuscripts is available along with subjectwise index, author index and alphabetical index of manuscripts.

There is a separate section for children between the ages 7 and 15. It is named as Vallabhji Ramji Bal

Pustakalaya Children can read books and can also play games like chess, Carrom etc.

There is a big reading room in this library, Students, scholars, can use this room by keeping a deposit of Rs. 100/- and a monthly fee of Rs. 20/-.

Reader other than students have to pay monthly fee of Rs. 25/- and a deposit of 100 rupees.

This library is open from 8.00 a.m. to 8.00 p.m. The library is located at K.M. Munshi Marg, Chowpatty, Mumbai.

8

BOMBAY NATURAL HISTORY SOCIETY'S LIBRARY (BNHS'S LIBRARY)

The Bombay Natural History Society at present is the largest non government organization in Indian sub continent engaged in nature conservation research. In the 124 years of its existence,[1] its commitment has been the conservation and sustainable use of natural resources for balanced and healthy development of future generations. The society's principle has been that conservation must be based on scientific research, a tradition started by late Dr. Salim Ali, the then president of the society. The Society, therefore, has a very well-maintained library.

The Library of the BNHS is one of the oldest and largest on natural history in the country. It has a collection of 20,000 books, 130 Theses and 5000 bound journals. Currently the library received 200 scientific journals. This is a **specialist** library having information sources on natural history, wildlife, ecology, zoology, botany and environment conservation. It has antique Shikar books and rare natural history lithographs of 19th and 20th century

1. It was established on 15th September, 1883 by 8 residents of Bombay (now Mumbai) in Victoria Albert Museum (now Bhaudaji Lad Museum, at Jitamata Udyan)

which are not available else where. It is a priceless collection.[2]

It also has a valuable collection of: Photo negatives, Coloured transparencies mainly those of late E.P. Gee, Dato Loke Wan Tho, R.S.P. Bates, M. Krishna, Dr. Salim Ali and those generated by the various scientific projects of BNHS. Thus, it is the largest library in the subcontinent to have such a valuable collection on Natural history. The Library has a large reference section too. Its reference collection has:

Gazetteers: Imperial Gazetteers, Gazetteers of Bombay City and Island, Government of India's Gazetteer of various districts.

Flora and Fauna Volumes available for reference are 'Fauna of British India' and Flora of India' They provide valuable information on biodiversity of the Indian Subcontinent. Besides these, there are Encyclopedia Britanica, Encyclopedia of Indian Natural History, Encyclopedia of Mammals, Encyclopedia of Environment Biology, Hamlyn Encyclopedia of Vanished Species, Encyclopedia on insects, birds, butterflies, turtles, fishes, trees and garden plants.

The collection of language dictionaries is accompanied by those of birds, scientific bird names, environment, ecology, botany, botanical terms, flowering plants, butterflies, moths and biology.

The reference section has valuable handbooks and checklists like 10 volumes of Handbook of birds of India and Pakistan, Handbooks on different groups of birds, animal, insects and flora of different countries.

2. Gurav Anant, *op.cit,* pp. 80-81.

Checklists are very important. They provide quick references on the fauna for natural history studies on particular region. There are various Checklists of birds, mammals, insects, reptitles, as well as plants of different regions in India and beyond. BNHS is affiliated to the University of Mumbai for postgraduate studies courses in Zoology and Botany.

Following are rare books and journals available in this library:

1. Insects of India' by E. Donovan, 1800.
2. Indian Serpents' by Patrick Russell, 1801
3. Oriental Memories by James Forbes, 1813.
4. Scenery Costumes and Architecture Chiefly on the Western side of India by Robert Grindlays, 1826.
5. Plantae Asiaticase Rariors or Descriptions and Figures of a select number of unpublished by Wallich N. (Ph.D), (Superintendent of Honorable East India) 1830.
6. 'Century of Birds from Himalaya Mountains' by John Gould, 1832.
7. Birds of Asia 7 Volumes by John Gould, 1850.
8. 'Parrots in Captivity' 3 Volumes by Greene W.T. 1884
9. Indian Ducks, Pigeons and Doves' by Stuart Bakers, 1910.
10. Game birds of India 3 Volumes by Hume and Marshal, 1879 as well as Stuart Baker's Game birds of India, 1921.

Besides these, there are several more rare books on Shikar, travel and natural history of the Oriental region.

Among the journal collection, the Proceedings of Zoological Society, London, dates back to 1832 and the Zoological Records are from 1890 onwards.

The library is mainly for the society's members. However, the library also caters regularly to information requests from scientists, Students, environmentalist and amateur naturalists.

Members can borrow two books at a time for a period of one month. The library provides a photocopying services.

Thus, the Society serves special and scientific research as its founders rightly aimed at.[3]

3. *GBCI,* Vol. III., p. 119.
Most of the information is collected from the members of BNHS and from its website : http://www.bhns.org.

9

BRITISH COUNCIL LIBRARY, MUMBAI

The British Council is the United Kingdom's international organization for educational opportunities and cultural relations. It is registered in England as Charity. There are eleven libraries of the British council in India.[1]

The British Council library in Mumbai was established on 18th October, 1953, at the request of the then, Prime Minister Pandit Jawaharlal Nehru.[2]

It was inaugurated by Justice Gajendragadkar. There were about 600 members and 6000 books at that time. At present the membership has crossed the figure 11000 and there are about 50,000 books. The Mumbai library is supposed to be the busiest. About a thousand members visit the library on Saturday. There are college students, students of Information technology and Management as well as students of other professional courses who take advantage of this library. The Library provides free internet service, and online services.[3]

1. They are at Ahmedabad, Banglore, Bhopal, Chandigarh, Chennai, Hyderabad, Kolkatta, Mumbai, New Delhi, Pune and Thiruvanantpuram
2. Deshmukh Shekhar, Dyanprasaranacha Suvarnamohotsav, Loksatta (Mar.), 22nd December 2003.
3. *Ibid.*

British council library has books for all. There are books on Economics, Engineering, Informative Technology, Law, Management, Medicine, Science and Technology, English as a language, Literature, Fiction, Social Sciences, and books for children. Thus, the library covers a wide collection of the written word.

Apart from the finest collection of books, the library has periodicals and Newspapers from the U. K.

Collection and Resources at a glance Books 35000.

CD/Multimedia	-	1350
Children's books	-	4600
DVDS	-	3000
IT Books	-	3400
Music CDs	-	1000
Spoken word	-	400 [4]

The library keeps in mind the changing needs of the people. The library celebrated its Golden Jubilee in 2003. It had arranged guidance programme for adults, competitions and workshops. It had organised an exhibition in Hiranandani Park, Powai, Mumbai.

This Library functions from Monday to Saturday between 10.00 a.m. to 6.00 p.m. It remains closed on certain public holidays.

This Library is located at British Deputy Highcommision, Mittal Tower, "A" Wing, First Floor, Nariman Point, Mumbai - 400021.

4. Library.britishcouncil.org.in

10

DADAR SARVAJANIK VACHANALAYA

Inaugurated on 23rd August, 1907, this library was first housed in Shri Ram Temple on Bhavani Shankar Road, Dadar, Mumbai. Well-known author in the Marathi language, Mahadeo Ganesh Gorey, had donated his personal collection of books to this library. The number of books went on increasing within a period of a year (1908), the library had 699 books, out of which 464 books were in Marathi, 216 books in English and 99 books in Sanskrit. Besides, these books, there were periodicals like 'Kesri' 'Kaal' 'Vande Mataram' 'Mumukshu' 'Deshasevak' 'Hindu Punch' 'Rashtravrata' 'Makaranda' and Patriot.[1]

As a result of this ever increasing collection of books the library was shifted from place to place. The Principal's house was not able to house the books. The first floor of the present building was completed in June 1929 and the new building was declared open for the public on September 8, 1929. After a gap of time, second floor too was added and the library opened its branches at Chembur, in 1960 and at Mahim, in 1977.

---

1. Gurav Anant, *Vishva Granthalayache,* (Mar.) p. 52.
   Principal Akshikar of Chhabildas Boy's School.

The outbreak of the second world war had an effect on the membership of the library. But the condition improved during the Golden Jubilee year of the library i.e., in 1957. The membership fee was also very insignificant, from 1907 to 1956 it was just 'six annas' and from that year it was increased to '12 annas' and then to one Rupee in 1966. On September 1, 1945 a special space was created for children in the library.

Earlier, in 1951, a separate section was created for rare books and other material for research work. Books an ancient literature (in Sanskrit) both prose and poetry, critics work on these old literature, books on History and other books required for post-Graduate students studying Marathi literature were also kept here.

There is yet another very important section in this library. It is named after Lt. Dilip Hemchandra Gupte. It has books on Science of war. There are more than 500 books on the subject.

In 1954, another section devoted to Hindi literature was created.

Presently, there are 80,000 books in Hindi, Marathi and English. They deal with different subjects like Economics, History, Political science, Pure Sciences and Religion.

Another attraction of this library is a special corner for 'Diwali Magazines' in Marathi.

The reference section of the library is on the second floor. It can accommodate about 80 to 100 people at a time. There are newspapers and periodicals in Marathi, English, Weekly journals, Maharashtra Sanskriti kosh in Marathi, Bhartiya Sanskriti Kosh edited by Shridhar Vyankatesh

Ketkar, Marathi, Mhani Kosh (Volume on Marathi proverbs) Dictionaries, Vyutpatti Kosh (Volumes on the origin of words) literature written by Veer Savarkar, Mahabharata, Dnyaneshwari, Bhrugusamhita, Tukarama's Gatha, 18 Puranas, Vedas, Upanishadas, Prachin Charitra Kosh, Jagatik Shashtradnya Kosh, book on World Science and the like.[2]

A catalogue of all these books is available on Computer. Separate section for students appearing for I.A.S. Examinations and a section for women are the two new additions.

2. Gurav A., *op. cit,* p. 53, *Loksatta,* 11 April, 2007.

11

DAVID SASSOON LIBRARY AND READING ROOM

The David Sassoon library has an interesting history which can be traced back to the Mechanics employed in the Bombay mint and the government Dockyard. In September 1847, the mechanics of both these institutions set up the Bombay mechanics institutes whose objects were to acquire a library, to establish a Museum of mechanical models, architectural designs and other matters dealing with Engineering and mechanical sciences and to promote the knowledge of these subjects.[1]

The institution was inaugurated by Sir Erskine Perry, the then chief Justice of Bombay who was its first President. It was first housed in the old clock tower over the entrance to the Government Dockyard at Marine Street, Fort, a stone's throw from the present site. Later it was shifted to a hired room in the Fort. In 1863, Sir David Sassoon donated Rs. 60,000/- to provide it with a suitable building. The imperial government donated a sum and leased a plot of 1485 Sq. yards on an excellent site at the Esplanade at the rate of Rupee one, per yard for a term of 999 years.[2]

1. Jewish Landmarks in Bombay and Thane, A. J. R. U, youth Group publication, P.20
2. *Ibid.*

The library has a large and airy reading room. Treasured within its sanctum are about 45000 books in English, Marathi, Hindi and Gujarati. There are some 250 rare books of 17th and 18th centuries. It also has Gazetteers of Maharashtra and other states of India. It is known for its collection of English literature and scientific literature.[3]

Besides enjoying the various amenities of a modern library like photocopying, computerized catalogue, Internet etc. members have the added advantage of a garden in the rear with shady trees and flower beds which create a relaxed atmosphere conducive to reading.

The library is democratically managed by a committee of 12 members annually elected.[4] There are about 2500 members of which 2095 are life members. The Annual membership is Rs. 500/- (Rupees five hundred only) and a member has to pay an entrance fee of rupees 150 and a deposit of Rs. 500/-. The library receives donations.[5] It spends about 70,000 rupees for buying periodicals, magazines, newspapers, journals, Indian and foreign and it spends an equal amount on buying books on different subjects.

The David Sassoon library is the third biggest library in Mumbai. It is open from 8.00 a.m. to 9.00 p.m.

The Gothic Structure of the library building has been listed for conservation by the government of India.

The library is located at:

152, Mahatma Gandhi Road, Fort, Mumbai – 400023.

---

3. Information provided by the library in response to our questionnaire.
4. Jewish Landmarks in Bombay and Thane, pp. 20-21.
5. Loksatta (Marathi Newspaper) dated 20th February 2006.

12

Dr. BHAU DAJI LAD MUSEUM'S LIBRARY

Dr. Buist, pioneered the Museum movement in Mumbai. In 1855 a museum committee was formed to establish a museum in the city. The government provided Rs. 6,000/- for this project.

In 1858, the East India Company's power to rule India was transferred to the British Crown and some eminent personalities of Mumbai like Nana Shakarshet and Dr. Bhau Daji Lad, wanted to welcome the new rule. They decided to build a museum, to be named after Queen Victoria. They collected a sum of Rs. 1,16,141 from the public. The government gave Rs. 1 Lakh and a plot in Byculla. The foundation stone was laid by Sir H.B.E. Frere in 1862 Later in 1975 to commemorate the death centenary of Bhau Daji Lad, the museum was given his name.[1]

The original museum committee had decided to attach a research library to supplement the museum. This library has a good collection of books on Mumbai city, (About 2600 books). Since these books are rare, they cannot be taken out of the library.

The library has manuscripts like Shahnama, Sikandarnama, Hatimtai in Persian. Besides these, there

1. Gurav Anant Vishwa Granthalayache... pp. 76-77.

are Sanskrit works like Upnishad sutra, Bhagvatisutra etc. The library is known for its collection on old maps, and gazetteers, dating since 1672. One of its prized collection is 'Malabar in Coromadal' written by Philip Beladeuce in Dutch, published in 1672. 'Oriental Memories' of James Forbes was printed in 1813. It is well preserved in this library. William Sheppard and Richard Bentley's book titled, 'Life in Bombay and neighbourhood' published in 1857, can be found here.[2]

Original books published in Marathi are also a valuable collection. e.g. 'Mumbaicha Vrutanta' written by Balkrishna Acharya and Vinayak Shingane. In 1889, it costed Rs. 2/-, Other book in its original form costing Rs. 7/- is 'Mumbaiche Varnan' written on the city's history by Govind Madgaonkar. Besides there are hundreds of books on archaeology, history, Indian art, museology, botany, numismatics, biographics, travelogues etc. It has all gazetteers, 35 volumes of Encyclopaedia Britannica, Asiatic Research Journals, Websters' Dictionaries, Marathi, Vishwakosh and other valuable material.

Secondly, the museum has kept articles on Mumbai city with pictures. Due to proper fumigation, many old books are still in good condition.[3]

The library is open on all days except Wednesday from 11.00 to 1.00 pm and 2.00 to 4.00 pm. This is a reference library.

---

2. *Ibid*. p. 78.
3. *Ibid*. p. 79.

13

FORBES LIBRARY

This library was established 1865 by Alexandar Forbes. He was very much interested in history of Gujarat, He had published 'Rasmala' a historical book in 1865. He was a judge of Bombay High Court and Vice-Chancellor of the University of Bombay. Keeping in mind his interest in History of Gujarat and Gujarati literature Forbes Gujarati Sabha, association to encourage publishing books, articles in connection with history Gujarat, Gujarati Literature, was established.[1]

Forbes library is Gujarati Research library. Initially there were 2000 books on different topics but mainly on literature. It has manuscripts and Gulabdas Broker's collection for research work is its pride. The library has a good collection of periodicals and magazines which goes back 19th century. The odd books are Unani Hakim Lokona Ahwal (1818) Sundari Tilak (1833) Bhartiya Jotish Chandroday (1819) Gujarati Bhashnu Vijukram (1839). At present there are more than 30,000 books and periodicals. Every year books worth Rs. 25000/- are added to this library.

1. Parikh K. H., (ed.), *Apnu Mumbai* (Guj.) p. 287.
The information is collected by way of questionnaire.

Life membership of this library is Rs. 2000/- Any one who is interested in Gujarati literature and history of Gujarat can become a member.

However, this is a reference library only and therefore, there is no lending section. It is open from 11.00 a.m. to 6.00 p.m. Research scholars, students and journalist make maximum use of this library. It organizes seminars (they call 'Bethak' in Gujarati) on literature, current literature etc.

The library publishes magazine called Forbes Gujarati Sabha Traimasik.

The library is located at 3rd Floor. Shree Kirtan Kendra, Opp. Utpal Sanghavi High School, Sant Gyaneshwar Marg, Juhu, Mumbai - 400 049.

14

'HELP' OR HEALTH EDUCATION LIBRARY FOR PEOPLE

This is a special type of library. It provides information on all health related concerns. It was set up in 1996 by Dr. Aniruddha and Dr. Anjali Malpani, two Mumbai based infertility specialists. It is world's largest consumer health library and first one to be established in India. The doctors who established this library think it is important to educate patients instead of just prescribing medicines. Their aim is to educate common man on health with information that is in simple and in common man's language and not full of scientific and medical jargons.

There is up to date collection of over 10,000 books on paediatrics, hypertension, fitness, nutrition, stress, eating disorders, and different other health related topics. It also has around 8000 informative Pamphlets, 3000 magazines and newsletters. The library also has about 500 videos that can be watched at the library in the audio-visual room. There is photocopying facility too. The library arranges talks on subjects like self healing via Yoga and alternative medicine etc. People of all ages can attend these talks free of cost.

The library is located near CST (VT) station. Previously it was at Om Chambers, Kemps Corner, Mumbai.[1]

1. The information is taken from an article by Priyanka Pereira in Mumbai Mirror, Thursday, January 25, 2007.

15

INDIAN MERCHANT'S CHAMBER'S F.E. DINSHAW COMMERCIAL AND FINANCIAL LIBRARY

This library was established in 1967.[1] From the time of its inception, it has been a major reference library. It is for the use of members of the Indian Merchants Chambers, business community, students and general public.[2]

This library provides selective and up to date source material on major economic, commercial as well as other developments in India and abroad.

The library has a vast collection of books, about 8000. These books are mainly on commerce, economics, industry, law, management, banking and taxation. These books are arranged subjectwise. There is a computerised catalogue of the books.[3]

The Library receives more than 400 periodicals. Latest issues are displayed for readers, so that, they can get information on current issues. Bound copies of important

1. It was established as a part of Diamond Jubilee celerations of the Indian Merchants Chamber. It was set up to etermize the memory of Shri F.E. Dinshaw, who was a leading industrialist and made a valuable contribution to the development of steel and cement industries of India.
2. Indian Merchants chambers booklet on its library, P.L. Members of the IMC can use this library free of charge. Others have to pay Rs. 500/- for referrig it for a period of one year.
3. *Ibid,* p. 3.

journals are also available. The library keeps a computerised index of important journal and articles for readers. Monthly Review of the Indian Economy, published by the CMIE is an ever in demand periodical. It serves interests of those who are seeking information on industry and finance.

The Library has growing collection of CD Rom on Commercial topics. Export Import data CD Rom is very important.

Newspaper clipping files are made available for readers. The library subscribes about 30 Indian newspapers. These newspaper are scanned every day and important items on topics of likely interest to the users are marked, cut and filed. The library maintains about 600 such files. These files are numbered and labelled in the following manner Computer Industry: C-19, Mutual Funds Mg, Environment: E26,

Such Files for the current year and of the two previous years are available in the Newspaper clipping section and are arranged alphabetically as per the topics. Thus, one file provides information on a particular topic.

There is a section of Directories. In this section there are trade directories from different countries as well as from India. There are more than 200 directories published by different associations, government agencies, institutions and private publishers giving information about industries, their addresses, products and production capacity, names of several scientific and research institutions, exports and imports, shipping and Joint stock companies etc.

There is yet another section devoted to pamphlets and brochures on wide range of topics. They are kept in different boxes as per the contents of the pamphlets.

Another section in this library is that of reports. There are 200 reports of committees and commissions, annual reports of Ministries as well as those of selected commercial organizations in this section.

It has several series of gazettes and notifications issued by the central government and the government of Maharashtra. Circulars issued by selected departments of government are also kept here. The library has a reading room, where, 50 readers can sit comfortably. It is open from 10.00 a.m. to 5.45 p.m.

This library is reference library, so one cannot take the material out. Therefore, the library provides Photocopying facility from 10.00 a.m. to 1.15 p.m. and from 2.00 p.m. to 5.15 p.m. It charges Rs. 1 per page.

The library has information search facilities e.g., (*a*) The computerised book catalogue and index of journal articles. Thus, one can locate books of one's interest or material on specific subject without loss of time (*b*) The library provides CD ROM based information search service with a charge of Rs. 30 for every half hour. For students the charges are Rs. 20 for every half hour. Print outs are provided at the rate of Rs. 5 per page.

The library has a unique facility of answering short queries like addresses and names of government and corporate officers etc. on telephone. It also answers queries received by post, fax or email.

The library intends to provide internet access for readers, facility of scanning clipping and pictures. It will also have phased digitization soon.

About 17000 people visit this library every year.

The Library is located at Resham Bhavan, 3rd Floor, 78 Veer Nariman Road, Churchgate, Mumbai - 400020.

The information about this library is provided by the (1) Brochures and (2) Response received from the librarian in response to the questionnaire given to her.

16

J.N. PETIT INSTITUTE

No Public Libraries existed in Bombay during the 18th Century. The East India Company maintained a library of their own as early as 1715. In 1804, The Bombay Branch of Royal Asiatic Society (then Literary Society) established its library, between 1804 till the middle of the 19th century some ten libraries sprang into existence.[1]

J.N. Petit Institute was one that was established in the later half of the 19th century. It started in a reading room opened by Parsi students.

On the 1st of April 1856 a number of Parsi students of the Elphinstone College collected a small number of books and housed them in a building in Mody Street, Fort, Mumbai. The Library was opened under the name of Fort Improvement library. In 1857, a regular committee was established to manage the library and the government gave it some financial aid. In 1866, the name of the library was changed to the Fort Reading Room and library. In 1891, N.M. Petit offered Rs. 25000/- in memory of his son, Jamshedji who was the Director of the Institute for many years. The library was given a new name again. It came to be known as the Jamshedji Nasarwanji Petit Fort Reading Room and library.[2] It was opened for the public on 1st May 1898.

1. GBCI, Vol. III, pp. 138-139.
2. *Ibid,* p. 139.

Accessible book stacks are housed on the original first floor of the library.

A Research Room houses several unusual and surprisingly novel volumes such as Kirtikar's — The Poisonous snakes of Bombay, Kaisarnama-Ki-Hind, a poem in Persian, dedicated to the British Queen Empress Victoria, written in 1877. It is illustrated with beautifully produced contemporary photographic prints.[3]

On the second floor we can find a free Reading room which can accommodate 450 readers at a time.

Thus, started as a private mutual lending library by a coterie of Parsi Students, today it has become a public library. Lawyers, law students, other students, journalists and research scholars make ample use of this library. At present there are more than 1 lakh books in Marathi, Gujarati, Hindi, Sanskrit and Persian. These are on different subjects like Philosophy, Geography, History, Law, Social Sciences etc. The library subscribes for more than 90 Newspapers published in India and abroad.

More than 4000 members take advantage of this library. The reading room is open on all the 365 days from morning eight to eight in the evening.[4]

The Library is located at the cross roads of D.N. Road and Sir P.M. Road, Fort, Mumbai.

---

3. Information received in reply to the questionnaire.
4. Information provided in reply to the questionnaire, Gurav Anant, *Vishva Granthalayache,* (Mar.) p. 32

   The Information is gathered from an article written by Rishi Majumder in Mumbai Mirror, Thursday, 18th January 2007.

17

JAIN SAHITYA VIKAS MANDAL LIBRARY

As the name suggests this is a special kind of library devoted to the material useful for studies in Jainism. This library was established in 1948 by an industrialist late Amrutlal K. Doshi. He wanted to learn philosophy besides running his Amar Dye Chemicals Company. There are volumes of Prabodhs Gita, Abhinandan granths which are long discourses on philosophies of various Jain Saints, Prashant Vayita, a Jain ritual guide book, ancient and modern Jain philosophical debates in Gujarati, Hindi and English. There are many papers, some of them are about thousand years old. Most of the books are published by Jain Sahitya Vikas Mandal. These books are waiting for readers. This is a reference library.

It is located at: 96 B, S. V. Road, Hirak Society, Vile Parle (W), Mumbai-400 050.

18

K.J. SOMAIYA CENTRE FOR BUDDHIST STUDIES LIBRARY

The K.J. Somaiya Centre for Buddhist Studies was inaugurated by His Holiness Dalai Lama on the 6th December 1993. It has been established to promote an indepth research and study in Buddhism. It was born in India but today, Buddhism is a way of life for many in the world around. It has a tremendous impact globally and is therefore, indispensable for understanding of history, culture, religion and philosophy.[1]

The Centre has been permanently recognized by the University of Mumbai for guiding students for M.A. (by research) and Ph.D. in Ancient Indian Culture, Philosophy, Pali and Sanskrit.[2]

The Centre's library was established in 1994 by the Somaiya trust and is financed by the same. The students of the centre and outsiders can use the library. It is a reference library.

The library had about 250 books in the initial stages, at present there are 5500 books on ancient Indian culture. It has original, Buddhist texts in Pali as well as their translations.

1. Booklet on K. J. Somaiya Centre for Buddhist Studies. p. 1.
2. *Ibid,* p. 6.

They have books on Manuscriptology and foreign language books such as Japanese, Chinese, Spanish and French.[3]

However, there are more books on Buddhism.

This centre and its library are located at Management Building, IInd Floor, Vidyavihar (E), Mumbai - 400 077.

3. Information provided by the Director, K.J. Somaiya Centre for Buddhist Studies.

Information is gathered by interviewing the readers and also from the plaque at the main gate of the building.

19

KAMALABAI NIMBKAR PUSTAKALAYA

The foundation stone of this library was laid by Shri. B.G. Kher, Premier of Bombay, on 30th May 1948. The people of the locality like Shri. Vishnu Nimbkar, Gajanan Deodhar and others donated generously, for its establishment. This library has most of the books on curriculum of different faculties. Therefore, it is widely used by student community. At times students themselves take care of it. The library is located at Khar Residents Association. 1, Chitrakar Dhurandhar Marg, Khar (W.), Mumbai-400 052.[1]

20

KUTUBKHANA MADRASA MUHAMMADIN, JAMIA MASJID

The centre of learning of Islam, Islamic Theology and Islamic sciences is known as Madrasa. It is never without a collection of documents. Each Madrasa must have Dar-ar-ilm i.e., House of knowledge, library. Maktaba Madrasa Muhammadia was formally started in 1903 in the premises of the Jamia Masjid, Mumbai. It was a part of Madrasa-i-Muhammadi, a leading centre of Islamic learning. Its collection grew out of donations from learned and rich Konkani Muslim traders, like Badruddin Qur and Abdul Qadir Jitekar.[1]

The library has books on different religious subjects in Arabic, Persian and Urdu. It has altogether about 4645 printed books and 1558 manuscripts some of which are:

1. Mizanul Hikmat on medicine by Abdul Rehman Khazim.
2. Unwanush-Sharaf on Prosody and Rhetoric by Sharafuddin bin Muqri.
3. Hashiyatual Alawi by the celebrated shah Wajihuddin Alwai.

1. Bijle S.M., *op.cit.*, pp. 81-82.

4. Al-Fathul-Mubin by Abdul Aziz bin Zaiuddin.[2]

Besides, there are some rare literary works in Persian.

The Iran Culture House, Mumbai 400002., has published "Bibliography of Persian Books" which are available in this Katub Khana. Even, Maulana Mohammed Yusuf Khatkhate, superintendent of the Mosque, had published a hand list describing briefly the entire collection then numbering 4851, in 1923.

The services of this library are lending and photocopying books and other material for students and researchers.

This library is housed in a separate building on the campus of Jama Masjid, Near Crawford Market, Mumbai-400 032.

---

2. *Ibid,* and also from the information provided in the response to the questionnaire. Information gathered in response to the questionnaire. The information is received in response to our letter to the Secretary, C.C.I. dated 5.4.2007.

21

LIBRARY OF THE BOMBAY STOCK EXCHANGE

It is a specialised library catering to the needs of Research Scholars, Businessmen and Chartered Accountants. The library has collection on books on Business Management, Finance, Business Law, Economics, Statistics, Company Reports and the like. With prior permission one can have an access to the library. It is a reference library only. It is housed in B.S.E. Building, Fort, Mumbai.

22

LIBRARY OF THE CRICKET CLUB OF INDIA

It is a library on Sports. It has a very good collection of books on Cricket. This library is meant for the members of C.C.I. However, if any research scholar wants to refer to this library, he can do so with prior permission.

The C.C.I. Library is located at J.N. Jala Pavilon, Brabourne Stadium, Dinshaw Vachha Road, Mumbai-400 020.

23

MAHARASHTRA STATE LEGISLATIVE COUNCIL LIBRARY

The first elected Bombay Presidency legislature was formed in 1921. The Legislators being new, needed references for drafting bills to make laws. So, a special library was established for them.

Presently, this library is housed in Maharashtra legislative council building at Nariman Point, Mumbai. This is a very well-equipped library with latest reference books, periodicals, journals, and reports of those commissions appointed by the central government. Some important works in this library are:

Legislative council report from 1962 onwards, Copies of State government Budgets, presented from time to time, Reports of various committees appointed by the state government, Gazetteers published by the government of Maharashtra and by the Central government, different types of constitutions of different countries, along with the election procedures of different countries, books on subjects like Religion, Social science, Economics, Agriculture, Industry, Health and on many other subjects, besides books helpful in making laws.

The library has a collection of Newspapers (about 80) and periodicals (about 150) published at District level, State level and at National level. The library also has newspaper clippings on important subjects. They are helpful to the legislators to get upto date information on a particular subject, when they have to answer certain questions in the house.

The library has a very important task of updating law books of the government by adding new decisions, by deleting the old copies, outdated information etc.

The people who visit this library include Legislators, Newspaper reporters, Research scholars, Government officers and authors. All can visit this library with prior permission. The library is computerised. It has facility of photo-copying, lamination etc.

The library has published 12 books of History of Maharashtra legislators, 1123 books giving information on the procedure of parliamentary government, 12 books containing memorable speeches of great leaders of Maharashtra and 2 books of information about notable legislators and 2 books giving biographical notes on National leaders.

24

MAHATMA GANDHI MEMORIAL RESEARCH CENTRE AND LIBRARY

This library started functioning in June 1964 under the guidance of Dr. P.M. Joshi, Dr. Gajendragadkar, Prof. Najib Ashraf Nadvi and Dr. A.S. Dalvi. Dr. Dalvi was its first Director. The centre has published about 10 monographs, children's books in Hindi and Urdu, and Mahatma Gandhi memorial lectures.

The centre has a collection of 40,000 books in Hindi, Urdu, Arabics, Persian, Islamic culture and History.

The library also has some old and important journals. A good number of authors and scholars visit this library.[1]

This centre and library is located at Charni Road, N.S. Road, Mumbai-400 002.

1. Bijle S.M., *op.cit,* p. 77.
Information collected from the institute's website.

25

MANI BHAVAN SANGRAHALAYA LIBRARY

This library houses most of the books related to Mahatma Gandhi. There are books read by Gandhiji or written on Gandhiji by others. There is a collection of speeches of Mahatma Gandhi, selected letters written and received by him.

Among the books read by Gandhiji one can see Layman's — What Christiantity means to me? There are books like his autobiography — My experiments with truth, All men are brothers, Character and Nation building, collected works of Mahatma Gandhi Vol. I to X. Constructive programme (This is available on line) Diet and Diet reform, Discourse on Gita, Essential work of Mahatma Gandhi, Vol. I Ethical Religion (available on line) Gandhi for 21st century by Anand Hingorani, Compilation of Gandhiji's Philosophy, Geeta according to Gandhi, Hindi Swaraj or Indian home Rule? India of my dream and so on. Besides these, there are books like Gandhi wisdom, The essence of Hinduism, The mind of Mahatma Gandhi, Village Industries, Village swaraj. The library has periodicals like Indian Opinion, Navjivan, Young India, Harijan and so on.

There are famous speeches of Gandhi Like:

1. Reception in Madras, April 21, 1915
2. Statement in the Great Trial of 1922, March 18th.
3. On the Eve of Historic Dandi March, March II, 1930
4. Speech at the Round Table Conference Nov, II, 1931.
5. Quit India Speeches, August 8, 1942.
6. Speech before Inter-Asia Relations Conference, April 12,1947.
7. Speech on one of the fasts January 12, 1948

The following letters of Gandhiji are available in the library:

- To Maganlal Gandhi, January 11, 1915.
- To Mangaldas Gandhi, after March 14, 1915.
- To Shankarlal, September 2, 1917.
- To Maganlal Gandhi, July 25, 1918.
- To C.F. Andrews. July 29, 1918.
- To Kasturba Gandhi, July 29, 1918.
- To Kishorelal Mashruvala July 29, 1918.
- To H. S. L. Polak, June, 27, 1919.
- To M. A. Jinha, June 28, 1919.
- To Shrinivas Shashtri, March 18, 1920.
- To Jamanalal Bajaj, March 16, 1922.
- To C. Rajgopalachari, August 24, 1924.
- To Kakasaheb Kalelkar, November 14, 1924.
- To A Friend, August, 1925.
- To Sarojini Naidu, April 11, 1926.

- To Lord Irwin, March 4, 1930.
- To Herr Hitler, July 17, 1944.
- To Churchill, July 17, 1944.
- To F. Roosevelt July 1, 1942.

There is also bibliography in which we find 100 volumes of Collected works of Mahatma Gandhi.

This library is for reference and is open to all. It is located at Manibhavan Sangrahalaya 19, Laburnum, Road, Gamdevi, Mumbai-400 007.

26

MARWARI HINDI PUSTAKALAYA

This library is run by Marwari Sneha Sammelan. It was established in 1916 with only 200 books. At present there are more than 30,000 books on different subjects like History, Novels in Hindi, Short Stories in Hindi, Biographics and Autobiographics Social sciences, Political science, Rural development, Commerce accountancy small scale industries, handicrafts, Geography and Tourism. All the books are in Hindi.

Besides these there are books in Sanskrit e.g. the four vedas, Upanishads, Gita, Vedanta, 18 Puranas, Sanskrit plays, Dharmakosh etc.

There are books in Gujarati also. A section of books in English is also found in this library. The English section has books on History, Religion, Philosophy, Occult science, Poetry Drama and so on.

Newspapers in Hindi and English are also subscribed by the library. There other periodicals and magazines in Hindi.

The library has been looked after by the sammelan and funds are provided by philanthropists like Shrinivas Bagadka, Madanlal Jalan, Ramprasad Poddar, P. Jhunjhunwala, Jaydeo Singhania and many others.

Besides lending books, the library also conducts some competitions for its members and gives prizes to the best literature in Rajasthani, Hindi, Gujarati and Marathi. It is called Ghanashyamdas Sarvottam Sahitya Puraskar. 1st Prize is Rs. 11,000/- and the Second is Rs. 5,100/-. Thus, the library tries to encourage young and budding authors.

One can become member of this library filling a form which costs just rupee one Rs. 5 as entry fee, Monthly fee Rs. 3/- (Rs. Three only) and a deposit of Rs. 100/-

Besides referring to the books and periodicals one can borrow one book at a time. The Library is open to all communities from 10.00 a.m. to 6.00 p.m. It is located at 227, Kalbadevi Road, Mumbai-400 002.

27

MUMBAI MARATHI GRANTHA SANGRAHALAYA

Though, there were libraries in Mumbai from the early 19th century, those who could read only Marathi had no special library. Hence, the educated elite of Mumbai established Mumbai Marathi Grantha Sangrahalaya[1] (MMGS). The activities of the MMGS began on August 1, 1898 in the hall of Brahman Sabha, Thakurdwar, Girgaon, Mumbai, with the four hundred books which were donated by the Bharat Yuvak Sabha.

A building specially for MMGS was built at Bhaijivanji lane, Girgaum. It was inaugurated at the hands of Maharaj Sayajirao Gaikwad of Baroda on 7th November 1912. By this time the number of books, periodicals and journals in Marathi as well as in other languages went on increasing.[2]

There was a great demand for a branch of library at Dadar, hence, the Dadar branch was inaugurated in 1941.

The Dadar MMGS is a very well equipped reference library for scholars. Many post graduate students, Journalists, Research scholars make the maximum use of

---

1. Karnik P. Ph.D. these on MMGS, University of Pune.
2. Lele R.K. Mumbai Marathi Grantha Sangrahalaya 1898-1973, Mumbai, p.1.
   Information received in response to the questionnaire.

this library. Some important books, manuscripts which are in the possession of the library are:

1. 877 'Dola Script', thcsc scripts belong to the initial (1800-1876) stage of printing. Scholars doing research in the art of printing visit this library, specially to see these scripts, and study its technology.
2. Robert Dramundans Illustration of the Grammatical parts of Gujarati, Marathi and English Languages, printed at Courier printing press in 1808 can be studied at this library.
3. Vaijanath Sharma's 'Simhansan Battishi', William Carrey's Dictionary of Marathi Language (1810) Marathi Bhasheche Vyakaran, Dnyanprasarak's Copies of 14 years are bound and made available for the readers.
4. There are manuscripts of Gangadhar Shastri Phadke's Marathi Bhasheche Vyakran (1836) Mama Varerkar's Work — Gharvali, Hari Narayan Apte's novel Vajraghat and great number of articles of A.B. Kolhatkar, Naath Madhav and other well known Marathi authors.
5. Other rare but printed religious books like Bankar Swami's. Saartha Dnyaneshwari (1907) 'Pothis' by Mahipati, Mukteshwar, Shridhar, and Vamana.[3]

Most of these rare books are donated by philanthropists and common people. At times, authors themselves, have donated their works to this library. Such books are kept in a separate section. Some important books in this section are:

1. Acharya Pralhad Keshav Atre's books
2. Poet B.B. Borkar's works.
3. Works by the poet Girish, V. S. Khandekar, Vinoba Bhave and others.[4]

The archives of the MMGS have old Marathi newspapers, Magazines and Weeklies.

It will not be out of context here to mention that in the year 1950, the MMGS had arranged an exhibition of rare books. At that time rare, 150 books were donated to this library by Tatyarao Savarkar. These books are made available to scholars for reference.[5]

MMGS conducts many other activities besides making available books, journal, and periodicals to the readers.

(In other words one can state the objectives of the MMGS as (1) To collect and preserve books published in Marathi and make them available for reading (2) To encourage authors to write and publish books in Marathi (3) To work for the cause of Marathi literature and thereby spread knowledge (4) To maintain a library of books published in other languages.)

MMGS educates masses by its following activities:

(1) Intellectual activities: Lecture series are arranged e.g., Dr. G.B. Phadke, Veer Savarkar Vyakhyan Ad hoc lectures. Round table discussions are held. Paper presentation, discussions, seminars, conferences symposium, colloquim are organized.

(2) Research Activities: Generation of reference sources.

4. *Ibid.*
5. 52nd Annual report of MMGS, 1950. p. 7.

Compilation of Bibliographies

Undertaking publishing activities. Imparting education and training and organizing study circles.

(3) Entertainment activities: Organising film shows, dance concerts to raise funds. But while organizing these activities all precautions are taken to see that no harm is done to the aims, objectives and philosophy of MMGS.

(4) Kalamandal activities: This Mandal provides platform to young and upcoming artists.

(5) Maharashtra Prabodhan Mandal: It organize cultural, scientific research activities, seminars and publishes periodicals.

(6) Date Suchi Mandal: This section identifies sources and prepares bibliography of Marathi books.

(7) Marathi Sanshodhan Mandal: It conducts research in Marathi language, acquires manuscripts, provides guidance to Ph.D. students of Marathi literature.

(8) Itihas Sanshodhan Mandal: It was founded in 1958 to generate interest in research in history, specially that of Maharashtra, also, to encourage the study and publication of History of Konkan, History of Mumbai, History of Freedom movement, History of the Peshwas. It has published 31 books on these topics. It has a Research Journal called Bhartiya Itihas. It tried to compile encyclopaedia of Mumbai but unfortunately this experiment failed.

It is a recognized institution for doctoral work in history. In this capacity the Itihas Sanshodhan Mandal had conducted orientation courses of two week's duration for research in history. It also collects historical pictures, artifacts and conducts exhibitions of the same.

(9) Sane Guruji Balvikas Mandir: It is for children. It has a library and conducts story telling sessions for them. It undertakes such activities which would bring all round development of the young.

(10) Ravindrabharati: To collect Rabindranath Tagore's literature and translate the same in Marathi. It conducts classes to teach Bengali language. These are the two important functions of Ravindrabharati.[6]

The MMGS was originally active only in the island city. Presently however, it has branches from Colaba to Borivali and from Thakurdwar to Mulund. About 20 small libraries are amalgamated in it. There are more than 40 branches of the M.M.G.S.

The Dadar library is open on Sundays also. This is a reference library.

6. Karnik Ph.D. Thesis.

28

NATIONAL LIBRARY, BANDRA

This library was established in 1917 by some enthusiastic group of young men[1] in a small chawl near Shriram wadi, Bandra, west.

They began with an appeal to the educated elite that whosoever, wanted to become a member has to contribute to the library stock, books worth rupees two only. The number of books and members went on increasing and the place in the chawl could not accommodate the books so the founder members went on shifting the library from place to place.[2] The Bandra Municipality appreciated the activities of this group and decided to give them an annual grant of rupees fifty. The society was registered in 1929 and the government recognized it as Taluka library in 1949 and it was registered as public Trust in 1953.[3]

The Bandra Municipality sanctioned 850 Sq. var. plot on 99 years lease at the rate of Rs. 2 per sq. var.

Information about this library is collected by way of answers to our questionnaire.

1. These young men were, Shankar Dhanaji Chirmule, Vishnu Dhanaji Chirmule, Damodar and Vasudeo Gangadhar Thakur and Dattatraya Shridhar Thakur.
2. From Ram wadi to Badam wadi to Nathoba Vandrekar's house to a block on Ghodbandar Road.
3. Gurav Anant, *Vishwa Granthalayache,* (Mar) p. 55.

The foundation stone of the library building was laid on November 2, 1948 at the hands of the then Chief Minister of Bombay, Bal Gangadhar Kher, The inauguration was done by the then governor, Raja Maharaj Singh. The Library celebrated its silver and Golden Jubilees. It has its branches at Bandra (East) established in 1975, Khar (1972) and Mahim (1975).

Altogether, there are more than 35,000 books in Marathi, 18,000 books in English, 5,000 books in Gujarati. There are about 20,000 books exclusively for the children.

The Bandra East branch has about 10,000 books and Khar and Mahim branches have about 7,000 books each.

There are about 4,000 members out of which about 2,000 are life members, even about 2,000 children are members of this library.

Ordinary membership of this library is Rs. 150 rupees deposit, Rs. twenty five as registration fee, and Rs. twenty as a monthly fee. However, the reference section of this library along with the periodical section are open for all, free of cost. A separate arrangement is made for female members in the central branch Bandra (West).[4]

The reference section has lot of valuable books like Henry Smith Williams Historian's History of the world's 25 Volumes published in 1907. 15 Volumes of the History of the world published in 1914, 23 Volumes of Encyclopaedia of Britanica, 2 Volumes of Transfer of power along with Gazetteers of different districts in Maharashtra, 23 Volumes of Mahatma Gandhi's literature, books authored by N. C. Kelkar, Bal Gangadhar Tilak, Marathi Dhyan Kosh edited by Shridhar Ketkar Marathi Vishwa kosh (15 Volume)

4. The information is collected with the help of questionnaire.

Pandit Mahadeo Shashtri Joshi's Bhartiya Kosh (10 Volumes) Chitrav Shashtri's Arvachin Charitra kosh, and other books. English reference section has works of Bernard Shaw, Shakespeare and others.

The Library's unique feature is that, it has books with autographs of well known Marathi authors like P.B. Bhave, Yashwantrao Chavan, P.L. Deshpande, Anant Kanekar, Vasantrao Naik, Shantanurao Kirloskar, Vyankatesh Madgulkar, S. N. Pendse, Jayant Dalvi and many others. Beside lending books, the library arranges Saraswati Kher vyakhyan Mala since 1951. Many eminent speakers were invited. The library's income comes from subscriptions from members, rent of the Hall, rent from advertisements and the government grant.[5]

5. Gurav A., *Vishwa Granthalayache,* (Mar.) pp. 55-60.

29

PARLE HINDU DEVALAYA MANDAL'S DHARMIK GRANTHALAYA

As the name suggests it is a library which has books basically on Hindu religion. There are Vedas, their translation in Marathi, Upanishads, Puranas, Epics, works of the different saints of Maharashtra e.g., Tukaramachya Gatha, the works of Eknath and Ramdas swami. The works of Swami Vivekananda, Ramakrishna Paramahansa etc. are also available here. One can find different 'stotras' 'Pothis' on aspects of Hinduism, Hindu festivals, Sacraments, rituals and so on.

There are more than 2,500 books in this library. The library is run by Parle Hindu Devalaya Trust and is funded by the same. It is free of charge. Those who know Marathi and Sanskrit languages, and stay in Vile Parle only, are given membership. One can borrow one book at a time for a period of 15 days. Every year about 50 books are added. Many people donate books to this library. The library is run by volunteers and is open on Mondays, Wednesdays and Fridays in the evening only. (5.00 p.m. to 7.00 p.m) The library is located at:

The compound of Parleshwar Mandir, Vile Parle East, Mumbai-400 057.

30

PEOPLE'S FREE READING ROOM AND LIBRARY

Peoples free reading room and library is 116 years old. This is one of the few institutions which provide free reading facilities to the public and also offers home reading facilities for nominal deposit of Rs. 200/-. Life Membership is mere Rs. 15/-[1] at this library and its branch at Shreeji Chambers at Fort. Students corner was recently set up here by Shri S.G. Chiniwala, one of the trustees. For a mere Rs. 50/- per month students can avail library premises for studying.

A free reading room and library was established at Revelin Street, Fort, in 1891 by Shri Damodardas Gordhandas Sukhadvala, He decided to establish such a library after reading the accounts of the munificent donations then being given by Andrew Carnegie in the U.S.A. for the founding of free libraries and Reading rooms. Though, by no means a wealthy man, Damodardas took up the idea of doing something on a modest scale to promote literacy and knowledge among poor classes. He therefore, established a trust for free reading rooms and libraries in Mumbai (Bombay of those days) He contributed by giving

The information is gathered by way of questionnaire.

1. Afternoon, August 4, 2004.

some land and an endowment, His idea was supported by several noted men of those times, including Sir Dinshaw Edulji Wachha, Sir Narayan Ganesh Chandavarkar and others, who became the founder trustees.[2] In 1930 the people's Free Reading room and library and the Native General library, which was established in 1846 were amalgamated.[3] The Native General Library was able to secure a permanent home in Framji Cawasji Institute of Bombay.

During all these years, both the libraries have catered to the people of Mumbai of all castes and communities by giving literature, ancient and modern. These libraries together have above 1,00,000 books. Some of these date back to the 18th century. These books are in different languages like English, French, Hindi, Gujarati, Marathi, Sanskrit, Tamil and Kannada. English classics based on Greek, Roman and European literature attract scholars. The star attract of this library is the complete collection of Punch cartoons. There is also a copy of Vachaspatya's Taratha Tarakachaspati — Three Volume Sanskrit dictionary published in the year 1873 in Calcutta.[4] Books on Swendenborg and Stoicism published in the year 1910, along with an old French translation of Homer's Odyssey are also among the library's precious collection. Besides these, there are transcripts of the Mumbai High Court judgements from 1890 to 1900. Valuable books on the earlier judgements in various districts of the East India Company

2. Anonymous, A Brief history of the people's free Reading room and library, p. 1. The first trustees were Dewan Bahadur K. M. Jhaveri, Justice Bomanji J. Wadia, Sir Ishwardas Laxmidas, Sir Purshottamdas Thakurdas, N.M. Samarth, and many others.
3. Why the terms people's is used? People's library was for the common people and started by the people unlike the Royal Asiatic Society that was more or less government.
4. Afternoon, August 5, 2004.

in the then presidency of Bombay are a treasure trove for the scholars and layman alike. Mumbai's earliest newspapers including Mumbai na Samachar, Mumbai na Chabuk are a part of the archives of this library. Cyclopaedias on religion, nature and other general topics are in good number. Amongst the ancient works, there are Babylonian, Sumerian, Persian and Akkadian scriptures.

Unfortunately the library has limited staff (Five including the librarian cum secretary and four library assistants)

Recently the library has revised its rates. To take one book at home, one member has to pay Rs. 500/- as deposit. One can read newspapers and periodicals by paying 250/- rupees as deposit. For availing the facility of reading newspapers one can get a pass by paying rupees 25/-.[5]

This library is located at Dhobitalao, Mumbai.

5. This information was given by the librarian in response to our questionnaire.
The information is provided to us in response to our questionnaire.
Information collected from readers of the Library.
The information about the Library is from its Website.
The information is gathered from Juhu library, in response to our questionnaire.
Information about the Library is provided in reply to the questionnaire.
Information is collected by way a questionnaire and from members of the Library.

31

R.G. SARAIYA LIBRARY OF NALANDA NRITYAKALA MAHAVIDYALAYA

This is perhaps the first institution teaching classical dance upto P.G. level as well as encouraging scholars to do doctoral work on dance. It is affiliated to the University of Mumbai.

The Library of this institution at present has 2,500 books related to dance and to the subjects like Music, Mythology, Philosophy, Ancient Indian Culture and Religion. Besides, there are books for general reading like Reader Digest. The library subscribes for more than nine magazines, Books on dance, in English, Gujarati, Marathi, Tamil, Telugu and Sanskrit are available in this Library.

32

RAMAKRISHNA MISSION'S SHIVANAND LIBRARY

Smt. Bhavanibai Pitambar Chauhan donated Rupees one lac for the hall and library on 21st September 1977. There are books on different subjects. Members are allowed to borrow books. Non-members can visit this library and refer to books but they are not allowed to borrow books.

The library functions from 5.00 p.m. to 8.00 p.m. and remains closed on Monday.

The membership fee is Rs. 180/- per year.

The reading room is open for all, free of charge, one can read newspapers, magazines and some books.

This library is at Ramakrishna Mission Road, Khar (West), Mumbai.

33

RUSSIAN CULTURAL CENTRE'S LIBRARY

The Cultural centre of Russia was established in Mumbai 32 years ago. It has become a living monument to the ties of friendship between Russia and India.

The centre gives importance to knowledge, education and studies. It tries to represent Russian Culture. Students get to learn Russian language apart from getting valuable information about Russian literature, day to day life of the people, folklore and also about the latest events in scientific and technological fields.

The Centre therefore, has a good library. It has more than 20,000 books on different aspects of Russian life. It is a collection of Russian classical literature and rare translation of Russian works into different Indian languages. One can also find recent editions of Russian periodicals and newspapers in this library.

There is a separate Art studio where there are catalogues on Russian visual arts, Sculpture, decorative arts, architecture, traditional and contemporary designs.

The Library is at 31-A, Dr. G. Deshmukh Marg, Mumbai - 400 026.

34

S.N.D.T. WOMEN'S UNIVERSITY LIBRARY

1. The Central Library is located at 1, Nathibhai, Thackersey Rood, New Marine Lines Mumbai-400 020.
2. Branch Library is at SNDT. Sir Vithaldas Vidya Vihar, Juhu Road, Santacruz (W), Mumbai.
3. Study Centres are at the above locations and Ratan Bag, Cama Lane, M.G. Road, Ghatkopar (W), Mumbai-400 086.
4. Children Library and Materials Research Center is at Juhu Campus.

The Central Library was established in 1955, where as the other centres were added later, The SNDT university was founded with the aim of educating women. Various social, economic and cultural facilities are provided for all round development of girls. This includes library facilities.

The Library System has the following educational material.

The information is gathered from Juhu library, in response to our questionnaire.

Information about the Library is provided in reply to the questionnaire.

Books	352713
Periodicals	963
Newspapers	41
Audio Visual Matenal	4876
Manuscripts	12
Thesis and Dissertations	4665
Annual Reports	2070
Reprints, brochures, Clippings.	17128

The Central Library as a part of Golden Jubilee Celebrations organised two seminars on Right to Information. A number of notable books were added to the main Library. Besides the routine, leading of books and reference services the central Library organised many other programmes.

The computerised catalogue is used by students, thus, making the girls aware of use of computers. Emphasis is laid on use of journals, and OPAC. Students use Newspaper clippings for their studies. The Library conducted 23 Orientation programmes of various types. This included modules on 'On Internet searching and documenting'. The Library complied 'Sahitya Suchi' the annual index and list of additions. Secondly, on demand from staff and students the Library compiled bibliographies on various subjects.

The Library organises and displays Smarak Trust Exhibition of reading material. These activities are conducted in all branches of SNDT.

35

SHRI ISHWARBHAI JIVABHAI PATEL LIBRARY

Shri Ishhwarbhai Jivabhai Patel Library is the Library of Narsee Monjee College of Commerce and Economics, Vile-Parle (West), Mumbai 400 056. The library was established in 1964 and the library was under renovation in 2006. The inauguration of the renovated Library took place on 7th March 2007.

The new Library is spacious (7400 Sq. Ft.) and well designed. The hall is fully air conditioned. The library has mezzanine floor also. The reading room has seating capacity of 300 students at a time.

The Wilson College library is an ideal traditional library and Shri Ishwarbhai Jivabhai Patel Library is 21st century library having 40 computers. In Cyber Cafe student can use their personal Laptops sitting at any table, since switches are provided for Laptops on each table. This is a fully Wi-Fi Library. The Library is also getting the new software of UGC viz. SOUL developed by INFLIBNET with 10 computers in network.

Information is collected by way a questionnaire and from members of the Library.

As mentioned earlier the library was established in 1964 with 6000 books, at present there are 30,000 books mainly on the subjects of commerce and economics. The Library also has Newspaper Clippings and journal articles indexing.

About 1500 books are added to the Library every year. Though, the library is for the students and the staff of the college, scholars can use it with prior permission.

36

SHRIDHAR VASUDEO PHATAK GRANTHASANGRAHALAYA (LOKMANYA SEVA SANGH LIBRARY)

This library is the result of hard work put in by people like Narayan Gopal Moghe. He visited almost all the well-known families staying in Vile Parle and collected books and by adding books from his own house he started this library. By the time the library celebrated its Silver Jubilee in 1948-49 there were 7000 books on different subjects in Hindi, Marathi, English and Sanskrit. Scholars like Mahamahopadhyaya Prof. Datto Vaman Poddar, P.V. Kane, B.V. Barerkar, Prof. N.R. Phatak, P.V. Gadgil, Anant Kanekar. B.G. Kher, visited the library at its annual functions. The people of Vile Parle thus, used to have feast of literature every year. The library is divided into three sections.

(1) Reference section (2) Gajanan Kelkar Children's section (3) M.C. Pendharkar Reading Section. Besides books, the library has a rich collection of Audio Cassettes of well-known Marathi scholars (Some of them are mentioned earlier), Marathi Natyasangeet, Shehnai and other instruments.

There are books on different subjects like History, History of literature, Administration, Political science, Economics, Dharmashastra, Management, Geography and Computer i.e., different aspects of Computer and Computer learning, operating of Computer etc. There is a rich collection of Marathi literature. There are books on investment, Agriculture, Animal husbandry, Horticulture, Medicine, Physical Education etc. They are made available for students and scholars as well as general readers.

H.C. Pendharkar Free Reading Room subscribes popular newspapers in Marathi and English along with periodicals. Every day about 250 to 300 People visit this section. The Library hours are 8.00 am to 10 am and 4.30 pm to 7.30 pm.

Annual fees for borrowing books is Rupees 250/- In corporation with Majestic publishing House the Library conducts 'Majestic Gappa' for 10 days in a year. This annual programme is very popular, since people get the opportunity to meet their favourite authors, actors, leaders etc.

The Library also holds exhibition of Diwali Magazines, Bal Jallosh Programme.

Members of the Library can go to the stacks. They can handle and feel the books. The Library staff is extremely co-operative.

Another important feature of this library is that, there are separate or special sections like — Savarkar Literature, Dictionaries and children's craft books.

Recently, the entire work is done by Computers. Readers can search for the books on computers.

The Library gives Special Prize in every two years for the best book on Indian Culture.

It is at Lokmanya Seva Sangh, Vile-Parle East, Mumbai-400 057.

37

SHUKLA'S MEDICAL LEARNING CENTRE'S MEDICAL LIBRARY

It is a special library as the name suggests. It was established by Prof. Ramesh D. Shukla in March 2005. He wanted to do something unique to help medical students. It is not possible for each and every medical student to buy books due to high price. He wanted to provide facilities like books, latest journals, CDs, Computer facilities to medical students.

If one looks at brochure of the centre it says, 'Read, refer, Browse, Study' — thus, it is a reference library, books are not to be taken out. It further mentions "Shukla's Medical learning centre has an electronic, library with continuous access to leading online medical reference materials like New England Journal of Medicine, Lancet, Circulation, BMJ Journals, Blackwell Synergy Databases, Science Direct, Elsevier Science Databases, Kumar and Clark, Harrison etc. Plus, Access to a broad range of interactive CD Roms and the Internet for online Medical Dictionaries, Databases, Encyclopedias and Glossaries,

1. Registration fee is Rs. 500/-, membership fee for one month Rs. 1000/-, fees for three months Rs. 4,000/-, for six months 7,000/-, Annual membership Rs. 10,000/-

Information taken from the Library Brochure.

The information was also collected by way of response to the questionnaire.

Information Resources, Clinical Databases, online Hospitals, Medical Education, online Medical Publications, Medical Forms, with links to Medical Databases and the Internet Healthcare Information Base.

This library has 6549 books dealing with 1489 topics on 78 subjects. It has 178 Medical CDs, 173 Medical Journals, 54 Online Medical Databases. All these are absolutely the latest editions.

It is probably the world's first ever independent library that provides reference to documentation that virtually covers the A-Z in medical learning. It is designed to meet all needs of students to prepare for their medical entrance tests. It helps assisting medical researchers and practitioners and para-Medical students also.

There are books on many subjects — Anesthetics, Biochemistry, Breast Diseases, Cardiac Surgery, Cardiology, Cardiovascular Medicine, Critical care, Dentistry, Dermatology, Ear Nose and Throat, Embryology, Emergency Medicine, Endocrinology and Metabolic Medicine, Epidermiology, Forensic Medicine, Gastroenterology, General Medicine, General surgery, Genetics, Genitourinary medicine, Geratology Gynecology, Haematology, Health care and administration, Hepatology, Histology, HIV and Aids, Hospital Management, Immunology, Infectious Diseases, Interventional Radiology, Laboratory Medicine, Medical Dictionaries, Medical terms and phrases, Medico-legal, Microbiology, Obstetrics, Occupational Medicine, Occupational Therapy, Oncology, Ophthalmology, Oral Medicine, Orthopaedics, Pain Management, Palliative Medicine, Pancreativ Disorders, Parasitology, Pathology, Pediatrics, Pediatric surgery, Pharmacology, Physiology, Physchiotherpy, Preventative and Social Medicine,

Psychiatry, Radio Rhematology, Scientific writing, Space Medicine, Sports Medicine, Statistics, Taxicology, Trauma, Tropical Medical Vascular Surgery, Virology and water, Electrolytes and Acid Base Disorders.

Besides this largest collection of books there are revision Aids for International Medical Entrance Exams Viz. MRCP, USMLE, PLAB and Indian PGCET. There is continuous broadband internet access to solve various online question banks like 123doc.com, Postestonline.com, onexamination.com, etc. for UK entrance exams and access to NBME and kaplan online question banks for us entrance exams.

Since this is a reference library it is open on all the 365 days and 24 hours Monday through Sunday. It is a very comfortable place of 4,700 Sq. ft. with 18 C room temperature and ambient interiors. There is pin drop silence and one can go to the open book shelves. Many medical students from Pune, Nagpur, Kolhapur visit this library.

The mission of this centre is "to meet the complete information needs of Medical students, the Medical faculty as well as the practicing medical fraternity and health professionals."

The library provides photocopier and scanner services for Reader Pass holders only. There is a special copier room. Black and White photocopies are charged Rs. 0.75/ A4 Size Coloured printout are charged Rs. 7.50/A4 Size copy. Scanning Photographs/books/journal are charged Rs. 25/- A/4 Size. Rare Books and material are not allowed for photocopying. Copyright laws are followed strictly. On- line Access, Sim Man Machine, Emergency care, First Aid, Health and Safety rule, cloakroom, Toilets and lockers, Laptop Computers coffee shop, Telephone services etc. are provided. The most attractive things about this library is there is night Membership. i.e., 9.00p.m. to 9.00a.m. which is free of charge.[1]

One can become member by registration after producing valid papers. Smoking and use of mobile phones are strictly prohibited in this library. Outsiders are not allowed to use multimedia corner.

This Library is located at 1st Floor, Brijbhoomi, Nehru Road, Vile Parle (East), Mumbai-400 057.

38

SIR DORABJI TATA MEMORIAL LIBRARY

Library of Tata Institute of Social Sciences (TISS)

The Tata Institute of Social Sciences was established as a graduate school of social work in 1936. It was given the status of deemed university in 1964. It offers master programmes in Social Work, Personal Management, Industrial Relations and Health Sciences. It offers broad-based M. Phil and Ph. D. programmes in Social Sciences and Social Work. It has programmes in Rural Campus in Marathwada also.

Sir Dorabji Tata Memorial Library is a unique feature of this institution. It is a library of national repute. It is well equipped with a good number of national / international journals in the field of Social Sciences. Its services are prompt and quick. The library provides service to university faculty, research scholars, students, private organisations so as to meet their basic needs in their field of studies. The library shares its resources and provides document delivery service with other libraries like International Institute of Populations studies, SNDT women's university, University of Mumbai, Nirmala Niketan, IIT, Shivaji University,

---

The entire information about this library is collected from the Website of the Institute and from the students who visit the Library.

Dr. Babasaheb Ambedkar Marathwada university, Fergusson college and many others. Information sources of this library are borrowed by such institutions and provided to their users. These services are made available by hand delivery, post and emails.

The library has compiled bibliographies on selected topics such as:

- South Asian Regional Conference future of Sociology, Social Work Education in India, Youth in India, A Handbook of Reference sources, and Ageing in India.
- Newspaper Clippings.

  This is a unique service provided by the library, News on Subjects like Aids, Women issues, Drug Abuse, Girl Child, Child labour and like are cut from newspapers and are clipped and maintained for reference.
- Online Public Access Catalogue (OPAC).

  This module of the library enables users to formulate their query and search with various access points — author, title, documents type, subject number and key words.
- Internet and E-mail service. This service is provided to all the faculty members and research students of the institute.
- CD ROM Databases : This facility supports academic research activity of Faculty and scholars. Some of the CD Roms are:

  1. Social Science citation Index, ISI, Philadephia (1997).

2. Wilson Social Science Abstracts by Silver Platter (1983-98).
3. Suchak CD-Rom by SNDT Women's University.
4. World, Development Reports (1978-96).
5. Business India and Seminar (1995-97).
6. POPLINE.

Taking into consideration the course contents, subjects taught and research needs of students, scholars and faculty has a good collection of books, journal of UN and other International bodies.

It has a small collection of rare books like biographics of social reformers, social reform movement of the 18th and 19th centuries. It has a collection of Audio visual Aids, Microfilm of books, microfichecopies of the census of India, Economic Times news papers in form of 35 mm film reels, 75 educational films. It has a collection of M.A., M.Phil., Desserational and Ph.D. Thesis. There are books of general interest and a small collection of fiction. The library receives about 300 journals in addition to a few of general interest.

Library Resources at Glance

Books (Bound Vol. of Periodical of Journal included)	1,03,350
Total No. of Journals	1,229
Rare books of special collection	65
Audio Visual Materials	1,600
CD ROM Databases	15

The Library also provides Information and Reference services, Reference Assistance, Telephone Reference and Electronic Reference Services. Telephone numbers for reference questions is 5563290-96 Extns. 282, 283, 284.

The library is located at Tata Institute of Social Sciences, Deonar, Mumbai.

39

SIR J.J. SCHOOL OF ART LIBRARY

Sir Jamshedji Jeejeebhoy donated Rs. One Lakh, for construction of an Art school. He was sad to see the pathetic conditions of Indian artists like potters, painters, sculptors etc. To patronise their art, he asked permission from the government, to start art classes. In 1866 J.J. School of Art began conducting workshop on fine arts. Later the school of architecture was also started.

A Library was established to preserve books, Paintings and Art pieces. Today, the Library is open from 8.30 to 5.30 p.m. On second and fourth Sundays it remains closed. Student of Art, teachers and researchers can use it. It is for reference only. Books are rare, costly and less in number. Therefore, the library staff has to keep an eye on all the readers.[1]

John Griffith was a teacher in this school. He was involved in the mural of Ajanta, which is the earliest work about the caves. In 1897, 'The paintings in the Buddhist cave temple of Ajanta', was published in London. A copy is available in the Library. There are books on paintings on canvas, oil paintings, printing, weaving, textiles, metal crafts, interior decoration, pottery etc. There are some works like 'The life of our Saviour Jesus Christ', Elements of

1. Gurav A., *op.cit.*, p. 87.

Hindu Iconography, Cochin Murals, and many more. Hundreds of old art magazines have been preserved here. Reports of archaeological Survey are kept. Besides there about 6,000 slides of paintings. The main problem in preservation is lack of funds.[2]

2. *Ibid,* p. 88.

40

Smt. JAMNABAI GOVINDJI, MAHADEVJI SMARAK TRUST CHILDREN LIBRARY AND MATERIALS RESEARCH CENTRE

This Library is dedicated to children. It conducts workshop for children during summer vacation. During Diwali there are competitions like story telling. The purpose is to provide entertainment and education for children. The membership is open to all. It buys books to activate young readers and develop their skills.

This Library is a part of SNDT Library at Juhu campus. It is also known as New Children's Library.

The Library has books catering to the needs of children from three to fifteen years. There are books and magazines like Chandamama, Balvihar, Children's World, Twinkle and Junior Britannica 16 Volumes, World Book 21 Volumes, Child Craft 16 Volumes, Tell me why 7 Volumes, Under water life etc. There are Bath books, which children can read while bathing. Cloth books are those which children can handle the way they want. Besides there are 3 dimensional books, giving information about human anatomy.[1]

1. Gurav A., *op.cit.*, pp. 96-97.

41

THE BHABHA ATOMIC RESEARCH CENTRE (BARC) LIBRARY

The Atomic Energy Establishment, Trombay (AEET) was dedicated to the nation by the then Prime Minister Pt. Jawaharlal Nehru on January 20, 1957. Later, Prime Minister Indira Gandhi renamed AEET as Bhabha Atomic Research Centre (BARC) on January 12, 1967 as a tribute to Dr. Homi Bhabha, the visionary who initiated the Indian Nuclear Programme and who was the secretary to the Government of India for the Department of Atomic Energy and who died in an air Crash in January, 1966.

BARC provides a broad spectrum of scientific and technological activities extending from basic laboratory bench scale research to scale research to scaled up plant level operations and its functional domain covers all walks of science and technology — stretching from classical school of thoughts to the emerging novel fields of interest. The core mandate of this institutions is to provide Research and Development support required to sustain one of the major peaceful applications of nuclear energy viz. Power generation. BARC also extends its expertise to chemical

The information about the institution is based on its web site — www.barc.ernet.in

The other source of information is Gurav A., *op.cit,* pp. 91-92.

processing of spent fuels, safe disposal of nuclear waste besides developing new isotope application techniques in industries, medicine, agriculture etc. Advance frontline research in physical, chemical and biological sciences are intensely being pursued in BARC in order to give nation a cutting edge in the field of science and technology at the international levels. BARC, thus is a multifaceted institution. Advance equipments and instruments, well-set laboratories, vibrant ambience and availability of expertise from all fields of science and engineering are the unique features of BARC committed in taking the nation to new horizons of knowledge and development.

Such an institution cannot function without a proper well-developed library. Therefore, in the central building at Trombay, was established a well equipped library and information centre in 1968. The BARC feels that it is its prime duty to provide scientific information necessary for experiments and that is why the library is an important organ of this institution.

The library buys books on Atomic science and Technology. The Librarian reads them and makes notes on the central idea of the books and keeps ready for the scientists. Since this library ideals with science and technology, most of the library staff is science graduate.

The library also provides information to international Atomic Energy Agency, Vienna, and to the International Nuclear Information system. The Library prepares index of important information (SDI), provides necessary information from science encyclopedias, translates important information concerning atomic energy, technology etc. which is available in German, French and Russian languages. Thus, the library has to do some intellectual job also. The librarians and other staff are given special training to search for such information and how to make use of the internet facilities etc.

This library and centre of information carefully preserves patents, scientific Journal Reports on scientific experiments.

In the year 1960, this library had more than 12000 books. But every year new books, Journals have been added continuously with the result that there are more than 100000 books in this library and more than 1600 science journals. These books deal with subjects like Mathematics, Astronomy, Physics, Science of sound, Electricity, Magnetic Science, Chemistry, Geology, Metallurgy, Bio technology, Genetics, Zoology, Botany, Medical science, Surgery, Veterinary science, Engineering, Robotics, Atomic science, communication, Mining, Computer science, Agriculture, Forestry, Management etc.

This library is very spacious. One can enter it only by showing identity card or entrance pass.

There are three types of catalogues and one can search for a particular book on computer also.

BARC arranges various seminars, conferences, lectures on science related subjects. The proceedings of such activities are recorded and preserved. Technical reports are also kept carefully. The collections of reports on Atomic science and Technology is one of the largest. They are preserved in microfilms, minofiche and films. There are more than 1,00,000 bound volumes of periodicals. The library has on line search services and internet service and has CD Roms. The Library provides photocopying service.

One can enter the library with proper permission and a security check. After all it is a special kind of library.

42

THE BOMBAY CHAMBER OF COMMERCE AND INDUSTRIES' LIBRARY

This is a reference library, situated at Ballard Pier. The Bombay Chamber of Commerce is an age old institution having been established in 1836. The library has annual reports of the chamber, Imperial Gazeetteers, Census Reports, rare books and many new additions are made to the library after 1947.

Scholars can refer to this library with previous permission.

43

THE HARE RAM HARE KRISHNA TEMPLE LIBRARY

This is a reference library, and as such books from this library cannot be taken out. This library was established by Shri Prabhupadji in 2001 and from 2004 onwards it is under renovation. This library has many titles in each languages and there are books in more 10 Languages. The library is mainly devoted to Vaishanvism and Vedic religion. The institution has Bhakti Vedanta Book Publication Trust. ISKCON Juhu funds and looks after this library.

This library is in the ISKCON Temple complex, Juhu.[1]

Information about the library is provided as a response to our questionnaire.

1. The Trusts aims at providing such facilities as photocopying, Internet, etc.

44

THE HERAS INSTITUTE LIBRARY

The Heras Institute was founded in 1926 as the Indian Historical Research Institute by Rev. Henry Heras, S.J. and renamed after him on his death in 1955, the Heras Institute, with its well maintained Library and Museum strives to fulfil the following purpose:

To promote Historical and Cultural Research in India aimed at strengthening an Indian identity

— in fostering study and research in the fields of Indian History and Archaeology, Indian Art and Literature, Indian Religions and Indian Cultures.

— in training scholars and teachers in the skills of Research Methodology and the Re-construction of History.

— in providing guidance and facilities needed for such Historical and Cultural Research and in collaborating with other scholars and institutions with similar ideals.[1]

1. Pamphlet of 'Heras Institute'.

Naturally, the library of such an institution is well equipped with original primary sources like manuscripts in Portuguese, English, ancient maps, the then contemporary works on history which are not available easily. Scholars can refer to the library by prior permission.[2]

The Heras Institute publishes Indica, its Research Journal since 1964.

2. Information collected by way of answers to the questionnaire.

45

THE INDIAN INSTITUTE OF TECHNOLOGY, MUMBAI, LIBRARY

The central library of IIT, Mumbai, serves to connect outstanding faculty and students to the knowledge of their disciplines, and thereby strengthens the aspirations and expectations of research and teaching work at IIT, Mumbai. The Library, is one of the largest in science, engineering and technology in the country. In fact, it is the knowledge hub of IIT, Mumbai. The library has an excellent collection of books, journals, and non book material in Science, Engineering, Technology, Humanities, Social Sciences and Management. There is a separate collection of Reference books, Standards, Pamphlets, Bound volumes of journals, Technical Reports, Theses study room books, Technology lending library and BC Book collection, Video Cassettes, Compact Discs and Microforms. This library is also a Depository Center for Indian Patents. The total collection of the library as on 31st March, 2005 is as follows.

Books, CDs and Videos	2,05,285
* TLL and Special collection	10,257
Bound Volumes of Journals	1,02,272
Reports, Pamphlets, Standards	66,124

* TLL - Technology Lending Library.

Photocopies/Films	4,604
Total Collection	3,88,542
Current Journal on Subscription	1,166

Besides these, there is a collection available electronically. The library receives 1190 periodicals in print including 1098 journals that are subscribed and 92 journals on gratis. The links to three files which have list of journals titles. They are alphabetically arranged in PDF Format. Besides these, there are electronic journals. Their list, alphabetically arranged is available on the web site of TLL Bombay.

The library subscribes to a number of important bibliographic data bases in the field of science and technology on CD Rom or through web. These important databases are accessible within ITTB domain.

E-Bibliographic Databases are:

Engineering Village Compedex

Engineering Village Inspec

Scopus Indian Standards

I Gate

Math Sci Net

ICSD: Inorganic Crystal Structure Database

J-CCC: J-Gate Custom content for consortia

PSYCINFO

All students, faculty members, employers and employees of the Institute are entitled for the membership of the library. Their entitlements, in terms of number of books that they can borrow and the permissible loan period is as per their position in the institute e.g., Teaching faculty, Emeritus Professors, life time achievement awardees, Research Engineers, Scientist, Librarians, can get 20 books for a period of one semester whereas, students of B.Tech (upto 3rd year) can get seven books for 30 days and so on Faculty, students and researchers from Government funded educational institutions and organizations are allowed to refer the library against introduction letters from their respective institutions.

The library is open on all days of the year except on Republic Day, Independence Day and Gandhi Jayanti. Its timing are Monday through Friday 9.00 a.m. to 11.00 p.m. and on Saturday, Sunday and holidays 10.00 a.m. to 5.00 p.m.

There are fixed timings for issue/Return of the books e.g. General Books, Monday - Friday 9.00 a.m. to 6.00 p.m and on Saturday 11.00 a.m. to 1.00 p.m.

The library is in the IIT Campus, Powai, Mumbai

The information is obtained from the website of the institute.

46

THE K.R. CAMA ORIENTAL INSTITUTE'S LIBRARY

This library is known all over the world as the main and most comprehensive sources of information on Zoroastrianism and Oriental studies.

K.R. Cama, after whom the Institute and the library are named, was an eminent oriental scholar, social reformer, educationist, linguist and a distinguished citizen of Mumbai. He passed away on 20th August, 1909. A memorial meeting was convened by citizens of all communities on December 8, 1909 at Framji Cavasji Institute, Dhobitalao under the presidentship of Sir George Sydenham Clarke. The Governor expressed his feelings about K.R. Kama and said "I am sure that we all feel that Bombay should possess some memorial of so good a citizen........... It is for others to decide what form such a remembrance should take. I will only say that I hope it may be possible to keep intact the valuable library which I understand he had collected and which must have played a great part in his life-work. Such a library, with the association now attaching to it, should not be allowed to be dispersed, and this, with other books relating to oriental literature, would make a collection of great permanent value. In conclusion, I will only say this, that the lesson I wish to draw from Mr. Cama's life, as I am able to understand it, is the power of moral courage."[1] Soon after this, on 12th January, 1910, there was a meeting of the general committee of the Memorial fund in the Town hall of Bombay under the chairmanship of Dr. Mackichan. It was decided in this meeting to establish some suitable centre for a collection of oriental literature, and of endowing scholarships for oriental research. At this meeting Damodardas Gordhandas Sukhadwala a well known philanthropist offered a sum of Rs. 1,00,000/- if a free reading room, library and oriental institute were founded in the name of K.R. Cama Thus, with this generous offer the K.R. Cama Oriental Institute was born. On 18th December, 1916, Lord Willingdon, the them Governor of Bombay Presidency inaugurated the Institute. The construction of the present building began on 11th November, 1936 and the building was declared open by the reputed Oriental scholar Dasturji Dr. Maneck N. Dhalla on 11th December, 1937.[2]

It is important to note that along with Mr. Cama private library, other individual and institutions also joined hands with the institute. They handed over their collections of books. Those institutes and individuals who amalgamated with the K.R. Kama Institute were:

- The Mulla Firuz Kitab Khana
- The Maneckje Limji Hateria Library
- Sir Jivanji Mody Collection
- Sir Dorab Tata Collection
- Dastur Dr. Darab Sanjana Collection

1. 75 years Platinum Jubilee Volume of K.R. Cama Oriental Institute, 1991, p. 6.
2. *Ibid.*

- The Jamshedji Unvala Collection
- The Behramagore and Tehmursp Anklesaria Collection
- Sir Muncherjee Cursetjee Wadia Collection
- Sardar Dastur Hormazdidar Noshiraman Kaikobad Dastur Collection.
- Dr. Phiroze Framroze Masani Collection
- Jehanbux Bomanshaw R. Vatcha Collection
- Irach Jahangir Sorabji Tara Porewala Collection
- N.H. Billimoria Collection
- Byramji Merwanji Irani Collection
- Mahyar Byramji Patel Collection
- M.N. Kooka Collection
- Siyavakshan R. Anjirbag Collection and J.D. Nadirshah Collection.[3]

With the collections mentioned above presently the Institute's library has a treasure of books and manuscripts of ancient Avesta, Pahlavi and Persian literature along with books on oriental studies. This library has 25,000 books 2,000 unique manuscripts on different topics related to oriental studies, 2,000 Persian books and 500 bound volumes of scholastic journal.

Following are some manuscripts and rare books available in the library.

R 55 - Vaetha Nask (Avesta & Pahlavi)

R 57 - Ithother Revayat (in Persian)

R 86 - Supplement to the 'Adal-i-Kaviye' of Mulla Feroze.

3. *Ibid*, p. 7.